...IS IT TOO MUCH TO ASK

...that the voices in my head
just agree on something once in a while?

BY:

SHAWN EAGER

Marginal Prophet publishing

ISBN: 979-8-9917017-0-9

...DEDICATION...

This book is dedicated to love and Patricia Anne, the woman who helped me understand the possible depths of it. There is no such thing (perhaps with exceptions for animals and children) as truly, absolutely unconditional love. But, we all want and are capable of giving a love that comes as close as humans being may ever get. In particular, selfless, healing and nurturing love that we all need to get by in this life and help speed our transitions along into the next. A very big thank you to those of you who are practitioners of such love. You are indeed the keepers of the energy that will, in time, change and save this world.

TABLE OF CONTENTS

...PREFACE...

If you have ever felt confused or even mortified by the direction of your own thoughts, this may be the book for you. This book (as suggested by the sub-titles) is a somewhat abstract compendium of my thoughts and feelings on all manner of things in this life set to verse, lyrical prose, or pondered in short essay form. I have never fancied myself a great literary mind, and this book may well prove me right.

I am also not a specialist in any field where one might consider my outlook or opinions a profound addendum to the humanities at large. I am also NOT a life coach. I am just another schlub trying to make sense of life on this planet we call home, the inhabitants, and our collective foibles. I will stake a dubious claim to being a philosopher of sorts... although perhaps "fauxlosopher" is more accurate.

In essence, we are all philosophers; if we have ever pondered anything that seems larger than ourselves...whether we actually find the answers or not is entirely beyond the point of the journey. The important part is that we search, we question, and we allow our minds the freedom to travel beyond our physical constraints. I would love it if this book feels more like a conversation to you than just a book of poetry and that you would want to add your 4¢ to that conversation. (...yes it used to be 2¢....but, you know... inflation)

I hope this book allows you to see that there is a type of freedom for your spirit when you allow your mind to travel, AND I hope that something in this collection leaves you inspired enough to document some of your own mental gymnastics to share with others.

With that in mind, and assuming you have indeed purchased this book, thereby deciding to subject yourself to this, my scrivened drivel, do not quote it as any sort of reputable source of knowledge. This may only serve to embarrass you in the long run and perchance, put me in the line of fire for a nasty lawsuit. And to be honest with you, my attorney and I are not as close as we once were.

So, thanks again, read on; I hope you have some fun doing so…and if this book, this conversation, turns out to have been of any help or inspiration to you in your own quest, I would like to hear about it. If you really like it please share it with others.**

You can contact us at info@marginalprophetpublishing.com

**(If, on the other hand, you think this book sucks, keep that shit to yourself… no need to harsh my mellow because you made an impulse buy that didn't give you joy. …but I will still appreciate your purchase…)

...INTRODUCTION...

How did I decide to write a book, and more importantly, what made me think I could get away with it?

Anyone who knows me would consider those fair questions. The fact is that there came a point in time when I realized I had no retirement nest egg or any real plan for retirement at all, and I felt I was growing older by the minute.

So, one day, I thought to myself, "...you know, with all the stuff you have scribbled down over the years, I'll bet you could probably write a book." In no time at all, I came to realize that since I was not an avid reader of books in general, I had no damned clue as to how to actually write a friggin' book.

So, there's that and the possibility that the voice in my head was drunk and was just goading me into this venture so he and the other voices could later have a great laugh at my expense. I know this is a possibility because a hundred years ago when I was barely pubescent, the same voice once told me how good I would look in a lemon-yellow Nehru jacket and love beads. Completely ignoring the fact that I was scrawny and painfully white, I saw Sammy Davis Jr. wear one, and I figured maybe I could pull it off, too. I did get double takes when I wore it, but the double takes were likely more out of shock than out of appreciation for my fashion sense. I mean, I was cute, well close to cute, well close to cute in much the same way that a spindly hound dog puppy is cute in a cardigan. Maybe cute adjacent is closer to the truth. ANWAY....

After having that thought about compiling a book I spent a couple of years mentally walking around in circles wondering how to do it, until I could practically walk the circle with my eyes closed. For all intent and purpose, I was walking it in my sleep, too. Then, one day, I woke up stupidly early for no apparent reason, but nonetheless awake...very awake, and very early, long before daylight, much less sunrise. Waking up like this was not altogether unusual for me. But this morning, I felt like there was something specific I was supposed to be doing, and I had no clue as to what that might be. I walked around in my robe and slippers (see Salieri Stabbing Mozart) for a good 45 minutes before I thought, hey, this reminds me of a poem I wrote once.

So, I went to my computer and looked up the poem. I read through it several times. Without a doubt, this poem hit home this morning. That is when I realized that this poem described many of my early morning quandaries. So there I was, sitting at my computer, hoping to miraculously discover some sign or some sort of guidance, or maybe even instantaneous editing skills…and I got this idea…

Beginning the following day, I would begin to take note of things happening around me and if anything happened to inspire me to write something new or perhaps reminded of something I had already written, I would start listing them on a day-to-day basis. (no…not every day; that would be way too much work…) Then I thought that maybe I would include a paragraph or two before each poetic offering explaining what caused me to think of it and again after in an attempt to finalize the thoughts. In that way, you might get a better idea of my cerebral operation.

I discussed this with a few friends, and it was suggested to me that this may be read as a journal of sorts if I kept track of the dates as I wrote. I played around with the idea of dating every offering as I went along. However the overlapping nature of inspiration to culmination quickly became confusing. I have included dates for the origin of individual poems and such. You knowing that the writing and compilation of this book did indeed happen in the order that you are reading it, over a four-month period; will just have to suffice.

In a happy, synchronistic world, you might find yourself reading a certain poem on a particular day when that poem was exactly what you needed to hear on that day…who knows, stranger things have certainly happened.

4

...AN EXERCISE IN FUTILITY...

This day, like many days for those blessed and cursed with a wandering mind, began far too early to be appreciated. On top of that, I awakened with a fair amount of trepidation for the day at hand, the places I must go, and those things that I felt obligated to deal with. Yes, I know that this domain is not my own. Almost everyone I know grapples with this anxiety from time to time. And while it is not a competition, I must tell you that for those of us who fancy ourselves as creators of some kind, we find these mornings where our day jobs rest heavily upon us from the moment we open our eyes, particularly disheartening...that is assuming that our day jobs are anything other than our art to be worked upon.

Imagine you're a kid, and you are given a brand-new box of Crayola Crayons, I mean the BIG box. You know, the one with the caddy, 152 colors, including metallic colors, sharpener and all. Now imagine having no coloring book to go with it. You don't even get any paper, and you know you're not allowed to color on the furniture or the walls...what do you do then? To me, it sounds like the perfect setup for a tantrum...

An Exercise in Futility   *(05/2007)*

...been awake since 3 a.m., finally rolled out of bed at 4...

...went to my desk, hands poised at the keyboard to write of my gloom and more...

...no lives are hanging in the balance, no evil here resides...

...but also, no joy, no peace, no sweet release for the art that quietly dies...

...my instruments feel like strangers now, my confidence eroding...

...no one who lives as long as I should feel their days foreboding...

...I know that I should live in thanks that I am living still...

...but my gratitude feels forced some days like I'm pushing it uphill...

...so I sit, I write, try to quell my spite, try to force my job out of my head...

...then frustration becomes my enemy, and I must fight that instead...

...Now I call upon the powers that be to once again fill my heart with song...

...to bring my muse back from the darkness where she has lived too long...

...I try to see beyond my frustration, believe that my time is at hand...

...the clock ticks away and reminds me each day that I am living as others have planned...

...I know that I am not alone. I know that others feel this way too...

...perhaps it's our hearts in congress that will eventually pull us through...

...so is there a communal force that as artists, we may tap...

...can we prove our intention to change the world isn't just a pail of crap...

...so, if you are reading this, my friend, you too awakened by your angst...

...know that you are one of many, and there's still no rhyme for orange...

...Damn it...

By the way, I feel we are ALL creators of some fashion. Some of us create in what the world considers "the arts." It could be music, dance, painting, sculpting, writing, basically anything that brings to fruition something that did not exist before.

But I also recognize the art in the creation of less grandiose things, what some people may think of as "mundane offerings." I can and do appreciate the art of creation in developing anything that previously did not exist. It could be a better filing system, a better way to utilize basic tools of technology, or creating new methodologies to improve on old ways of doing things. Even finding a new way to use traditional tools in a workshop or creating order from chaos in an office, a construction site, a classroom, in homemaking and parenting, all of them are creations, works of art born of skill and concentration, and sometimes divine intervention.

No matter what your daily routines offer up, you could be in a position to occasionally create a little something better for yourself, your family, your employer, or maybe even just for someone you love or care for. Not all creations are strokes of genius in monumental proportions. Smaller creations can still be considered genius, too. And you may never know whose life you might improve with your particular insight.

...A GRACEFUL BOW...

Today, while I was at the grocery store, I had a few thoughts. I was shopping from a list I had made hours before, so my mind was free to wander as I schlepped my way through the isles of poor food choices in bright and smartly designed packaging. I mean, I created my list based on actual need with the use of the ad flyer that came in the mail the day before. I was determined not to buy what I did not need. Well, we all know how seldom that works flawlessly. It is almost a foregone conclusion that I will purchase something I don't need, rationalizing it as a treat for myself for not giving in to the temptation to buy a bunch of stuff I didn't need. Does anybody else recognize this clearly ridiculous circle of behavior?

Anyway, there I was, performing another relatively mindless task. I have performed this very task for years, the only difference being that in years gone by, I would be doing this for my family, my wife, and my kids. Now, in what is said to be my golden years, I do this for me alone. My wife has passed, and my kids have families of their own. Now with plenty of time to think about just me, I find that I don't really know how to think about just me. I began to realize that for much of my adult life, I let myself think that my daily routines were my life. That included whatever I was doing for a living at the time.

When you meet someone new, invariably, one of the topics of conversation is answering the question, "...so, what do you do for a living?" At some point in time, I began to understand that what I do is not necessarily who I am. God bless those who earn their living doing what they truly love. For them, those two things are inclusive of one another, but not for most of us. So, as I made my way around the store, pushing my cart with the one uncooperative wheel, I began to think about how often I failed to notice time slipping by. I began to see how often I was not much more than a supporting role in a myriad of other people's lives. And I wondered if I could learn to be an appropriately selfish man and wondered if that change would give others in my life any cause for concern or if my newly unwrapped selfishness would just piss them off.

What happens from this point on is a new direction for me. Maybe some of you reading this will see some of yourself in this quandary, too. I intend to be much more aware of time's passing. I will not obsess over it because that would be a waste of time... again, does anybody else recognize this as a vicious circle? Funny how this becomes more important the older you get.

A Graceful Bow   *(09/2020)*

I've been waiting, and I don't know why,
I think I've been standing in my own way,
afraid to even try

Long overdue is this change I seek, and I have a lot to say,
It's time to toss it to the wind and hope it finds its way

To the persons who may need to hear it most,
Perhaps some persons who have lived their lives as little more than ghosts

A voice in my head suggests it's time to be the lead in my own stories,

Because supporting roles grow tiresome and garnish little glory

It seems I've been planning for years now...

just without a real plan,

walking around in circles with keys here in my hand

Spinning down a hallway that is filled with unmarked doors,

Afraid to even try the locks that just might lead to more

I wonder if I fear failure, or do I fear I might succeed,

I suppose either way is still movement, and movement is what I need

Do you, like me, want to take control, change your story line by line,

Be the playwright and director and the star while there is time.

Well, even when you feel uncertain about the story or the timing

Maintain your gaze toward the end you desire, and seek the silver lining

Does this sound like you? Are you like me? Are you standing in the wings,

Watching as the play unfolds and noticing odd things

Are you seeing people being less like themselves than they used to be,

Are you seeing larger spaces between what is and what should be?

I used to feel I was not worthy of the changes I desired,

I used to think it was too much work, and I was already tired

But now I see I am allowed to want as long as I'm not a greedy fool

I must want the same for others in this world. I must be selfish FOR the needy, too.

So if you, like me, want to change your world, don't try to fix all the world got wrong,

Vow to change what may be stopping you, and your world will change before long.

Am I a font of knowledge? No, just a searching, soulful toad,

And I'll share MY truth as I find it while I stumble down this road

I'll be trying all the keys now until I find the door and see what's inside.

I'll no longer shy away from change; I think that's where the blessings hide.

This poem is an example of my admonishment to myself; my conscience told me sharing that is something I should do

So, too, my mea culpa, a penance in itself, a purging of the doubt to let the miracles come through

A journey to find oneself again only guarantees a search and not a solution.

But every step and misstep along the way is still part of the evolution.

You're allowed to be confused sometimes; you're allowed to have bad days

You're allowed to forgive yourself if, sometimes, your gratitude slips away

You're allowed to focus on happiness, you're allowed to focus on love,

You're allowed to gift yourself the peace that you've been dreaming of

Look no further if you seek permission; you're allowed to change your life,

You're allowed to say yes to bliss and allowed to say no to the strife

You're allowed to drop old baggage, bid days gone by a fond farewell,

make a graceful bow to your old life, lift your skirt, and run like hell…

So, those were my thoughts for this day, very similar to thoughts I've had before and I'm certain to have them again. These are the thoughts we all must entertain, maybe daily, if we are to separate "making a living" from "making a life." I'll assume you have already determined that I spend a bit of time contemplating my purpose in this life. That too, seems to happen more often the older I get. I will be addressing these thoughts and others throughout this book. But have no fear. I will also be addressing other occasionally confusing notions that seem to be at battle with one another, like need versus want, spirituality versus religion, and love versus lust. I'm sure as the writing of this book continues, I will discover plenty of other paradoxical comparisons to contend.

...SHOULDA-COULDA-WOULDA...

I'm going to share with you some hard discoveries about myself throughout this collection of thoughts. The reality is that I have tried for years to figure out what it is that nags at me to be said and how to say it. Among other things, I fancy myself as a singer/songwriter. That is where writing began for me, and I did not truly find my voice until I was in my early forties. So, writing has been my avocation for well over twenty-five years and to date, precious few people have actually had the chance to hear what I've tried to say. That is no one's fault but my own. I spent way too much time trying to be perfect with everything I wrote and not trusting the message itself.

But once I realized that I was fast approaching retirement age, with no retirement plan and that some medical situations may speed that up, I began to feel pressured to document my thoughts, haphazard though they may be. Whether the thoughts were large or small, obvious or not, insightful or not, hopeful, sarcastic or just plain silly did not make a difference to me. I was going to start writing and then try to determine what portions of my synaptic ramblings might have value to anybody else. So, I started writing not just more songs but poetry, prose, and short essays as well. I even started jotting down one and two-line philosophical thoughts. (from this point forward, I will refer to those as fauxlosophy because I have no formal training of any sort that would grant me a title as a philosopher).

I began writing what I thought might become a blog or a series of "snackable" videos, small by nature but still enough meat to be satisfying to some degree. People say to write about what you know. Well, here is one thing I know... I know I am ill-prepared for retirement. Twice during my lifetime, my meager savings had to be exploited to keep up with bills due to accidents, illnesses or stints of unemployment. So I thought, okay then, I'll write about that, how to survive in that scenario.

I quickly realized that all I had to offer with regard to that would be an introspective of shortcomings and bad planning, and that certainly sounds helpful…right? Anyway, some of what would come from that does have some value because of the soul-searching it provided, and I will share some here and there. Who knows, maybe by the time I finish this book I will have become organized enough to actually make those videos. I only include this now because it IS about the beginning of this journey. If/when it happens, it will have been doled out in parts.

Here is part one.

Shoulda-Coulda-Woulda… *(07/2020)*

(the enigma of knowing I do not know how much I do not know)

I have always seen myself as sort of a renaissance man, but at the same time always questioned my self-image. I see myself as a decent singer/songwriter, artist, designer, wood crafter, poet, cook…. all that "renaissance man" hoopla. So, with all I have to offer, why am I not swimming in money, fame, and influence? Why am I not yet enjoying the wonderful things in my life we all dream about and hope for?

Is it because I am not the best at any one thing…no, of course not. Clearly, there are scads of people creating great works of mediocrity who are doing well for themselves.

Is it because I didn't work hard enough…again, no. I have worked very hard in my life, and there are people who, as amazing as it seems, do very well with minimal effort. I fail to understand the equity of such things, but there you are.

Is it because I have not suffered enough for my art…still…no. Must I live in abject poverty, succumb to some respiratory disease, or lop off a body part to prove my dedication…. uh, no.

The facts are that not everything in this life is automatically equitable; the unexpected happens and life has a way of slowing you down. And if you allow it to slow you down too much, you'll eventually come to a stop; you know all that "an object in motion stuff...". The reality is that principle is not only true in the physical world, but also in the metaphysical world and in the ever-shrinking space between the two.

There is also a deceptively simple factor at play, a question really. That question is so basic that it escapes notice in most cases. That question is the beginning of the journey and requires one to be absolutely honest with themselves in answering it. Finding the strength to answer this question with a resounding and steadfast YES is the first step in attacking all other questions and setbacks in a journey to build your life as you wish it to be. It is a cold fish-to-face question that needs to be answered at the start....am I ready? That's it, that is the question. Am I ready for a new life ripe with opportunities and surprises? Am I ready to step outside of my hard-earned comfort to obtain that which I tell myself I really want? Am I ready, or do I in some way fear success because it would mean major changes in my life? Am I ready, or do I in some way fear failure because it could cost me some of my comfort? Am I ready to accept possible failure, maybe more than a few times, to achieve the end goal? ... Am I ready? ...Are you?

There you have it, a confession of sorts to being ignorant of the processes required AND being a procrastinator by nature. I'm finding procrastination tougher to beat than my nicotine addiction was. But that is what this collection of thoughts and the "day-to-day" approach is all about. I do not make New Year resolutions; in fact, I rarely promise myself anything. But clearly, forward progress relies on change and some kind of commitment to it. That means along with all the other changes I tell myself I will make, I now add R&D for digital media purposes and kick the procrastination habit. This is starting to feel like an AA meeting or something… Hi, my name is Shawn, and I'm a procrastinator… I think if there were such a group as Procrastinators Anonymous, it would likely fail in short order. Most of the potential members would just put off going to the meetings.

...WISHES...

I have two cats. I did not choose to have two cats. There was a period of time when two of my granddaughters were living with me and my wife. My wife rightfully surmised that these girls needed something to love. You see, love is meant to be a two-way street, a balance between give and get. And with these girls, it worked; the cats became their "give." Long story short, the girls moved out, and the new home did not allow pets, so my wife and I ended up with two cats. My wife has passed... now I have two cats...

So, last night, I went to bed at a reasonable hour; by that, I mean before midnight. I slept well for all of four and a half hours before my cat started walking on me and gently meowing as if to say, "...please wake up. There is something that needs your attention." Because this animal is not usually very vocal, I assumed he was truly in need of something. I begrudgingly got up, put on a robe and followed him out to the kitchen. He went straight to the back door, so I naturally gleaned that he needed to go out and manage some business.

I opened the door, he adopted a most peculiar-looking physical attitude and stood there looking out into the darkness as though he expected dragons or aliens to come rushing in. I asked him if he was going to go out or not, and he responded by sitting down and staring at me.

I closed the door, admonished him for being so non-committal and decided to go back to bed. Now, mind you, he had played this game before, where as soon as I walked away from the back door, he would run to it and scratch at the jamb to go out. The second time is the charm...stupid cat.

This time, however, as I turned to leave the kitchen, he ran in front of me, damn near causing me to trip over him. I stopped, then he reached up with one paw and grabbed the bottom of my robe as if to say, "...here...you need to be here...".

17

I looked at him, he looked at me, I looked around; food-check, water-check, no snakes, dragons, aliens or cucumbers-check. I asked him, this time with little patience left, "What do you want, cat?" Still clinging to my robe, he looked at his food bowl, then at me, then again at the food bowl. Apparently, because he could see the bottom of his bowl at its center, he was concerned.

"Seriously?" I said, "This is what has your knickers in a bunch?" I nudged the bowl with my foot, causing the kibble to shift, thereby covering up the previously visible white ceramic bottom. He looked at the bowl, looked at me, looked at the bowl again, released his grip on my robe and began eating. I was miffed. I told him again how stupid he was and turned to go back to bed. One step away and he ran straight to the back door where he proceeded to reach for the jamb. "You little prick," I said as I opened the door and pushed him outside. I stood there looking at him from the pass-through window of the back door, thinking I have rarely loved and hated something so much at the same time. Who's the stupid one now?

Wishes *(08/17)*

I got a big white dog. He's got big white balls

He lays around the house all day don't do nothing at all

Uh-huh… Uh-huh…

Uh-huh…I wish I was a big white dog.

I got a mean old cat that I still feed.

But when he come around lookin' for affection, he gets all of that he needs,

Uh-huh… Uh-huh…

Uh-huh...I wish I was a mean old cat.

I got a rooster bird, struts and crows all night,
Don't even think about goin' to sleep until just before daylight,
Uh-huh... Uh-huh...
Uh-huh...I wish I was a rooster bird.

I got an old milk cow; she doesn't milk anymore
Been cut up long ago, except my wife loves that cow for sure,
Uh-huh... Uh-huh...
Uh-huh...I wish I was an old milk cow.

I have a brother-in-law who lives in my spare room
Spends all his money on whiskey, and women ain't got jack when the rent comes due
Uh-huh... Uh-huh...
Uh-huh...I wish that man would leave.

Uh-huh... Uh-huh...
Uh-huh...I wish wishes could come true.

There you have it, just another passive-aggressive love story. I said before that I have rarely loved and hated something so much at the same time, but I was married for 48 years. Don't get me wrong, I loved that woman with a passion all of that time, but like any other long-term relationship, there will be those moments. Not the moments that test your love per-say, but the moments where you question whether you still like them or not. My life experiences have left me to believe that once you grow to love something, you can still love it even if it irritates you sometimes,

19

and yes, even after it has outlived the major life expectancy of its usefulness.

I only hope that once I have outlived the better part of my usefulness to this weary world, my contributions to life, in general, will have been enough to warrant my sticking around and being loved, even if I am irritating from time to time. I mean, I was blessed with a very long and loving marriage. I was blessed with four healthy children, all of whom I let live to eventually be blessed and cursed with kids of their own.

Uh-huh… Uh-huh…

...THE MARVELOUS PROCRASTINATOR...

Here we are at the relative beginning of this book, and I have already sought a little input from a friend whom I consider quite literate, meaning dozens of years ago, she majored in English Literature. When I asked for her opinion on what I was doing, she informed me that it was an interesting blend of poetry, philosophy, and stream-of-consciousness writing. I thanked her for her input and went on my merry way, but with more questions, I should have asked her at the time. But I did not ask her because I hate to appear ignorant without some kind of warning that my ignorance may be expected on any given topic. Let's face it: if the topic had been string theory, my lack of knowledge would be pretty much expected. But because the Q&A was about writing, something I have been doing for years, I was not about to let my ignorance show, at least not at that moment.

The poetry part was obvious to me, so to the fauxlosophy part, I mean that was the whole nature of this entire enterprise, to begin with, but the stream of consciousness thing...? You see, I lost interest in reading for fun shortly after high school, as most of my reading became job oriented. So, precious few novels, and to my knowledge, I had never read anything where this style was used. I had heard of it but did not know what it actually was. What follows is something I wrote a few years ago. I thought this is what stream-of-consciousness writing was...turns out, not so much. This only proves the old adage, "A little knowledge can be a dangerous thing," or, in my case, a ridiculous thing.

The Marvelous Procrastinator   *(11/2020)*

(an exercise in "real-time writing")

So, ...there I was, in my house, in the room that has been purported to be a "studio/office." I could take actual pictures to share with you, but that could make this embarrassment all too real. I may, however, post some kind of before and after photo or video once I determine what this dissertation is actually about. But probably not; I am a well-known procrastinator. It will be most helpful if there is then found an end on which to report as well, but we shall see. I will describe for you, "the room" as I view it from my swiveling office chair, clockwise around the room. I may also report to you the memories of successes and/or failures, as suggested to me by the clutter that surrounds me. I do not know how long this willingness will last; I assume until I can bear it no more.

__me__...Oh my God, are you really going to do this? Are you going to "write in the moment?" You're really going to regurgitate all the crap that floats through your head as you TRY to create a random work of genius that will just magically contain some socially redeeming qualities?

__also me__... WHY NOT, we're already sitting in the damn chair, aren't we?

__me__... Man, if I find out that this writing-in-the-moment thing doesn't work when you're sober, I will be quite put out...

__also me__... or so you say...

So, ...there I was, in my house, in "that" room, sitting at my desk, fingers poised over my keyboard as if I were going to stab the words onto the page. I have every intention of writing something uplifting. (...yeah...uplifting...) I sat and looked around the room. I looked at all the stuff I've amassed to help myself, and I still find myself lacking. The lack is not, however, physical. There are books and other tools all around me with which to wheedle my muse and her creativity out of its hiding spot.

It was about that time that I realized I still have not learned to actually use all of these tools I own. Then I had this thought: I wondered what made me such a terrible procrastinator and what makes me act the way I do. Let me rephrase that...I often wonder what made me such a remarkable procrastinator.

__Me__...you see what I did there ?... I phrased that so the adjective kindly leaves it up to the reader to decide upon the appropriate definition for the word "remarkable" based only-y-y-y on-n-n ...that's right,...what I decide to tell them. That sounds fair...right?

__Also, me__...to be blunt, no. But we're not really interested in fairness right now...are we?

Okay then, nod your head if you think that just sounded like I might get edgy or political... and then maybe buckle up. For those of you who may be nodding now, keep nodding slowly; there's more. Now place your hand (or hands if you happen to be so fortunate) in your lap, palms up to the heavens. Relax your shoulders, and try to focus on the movement of your neck. Try to achieve an almost liquid motion. This may help; everyone starts the nodding action with the briefest of nods upwards before sharply bringing the head back down for the full nod. So, stop nodding for a moment. Face forward and slowly tuck your chin down toward your chest. As you bring your head upward, note that you lead that motion with your nose and your chin moving ever so slightly forward as you lift your face and head. Do it a few times until you can feel that slight elliptical motion to the movement. Do it a few more times. Now close your eyes...

__Also, me__...hey, if you are reading this, instead of nodding your head up and down with your eyes closed...well done. You may survive at least part of the future purge of humanity...

Okay, back to it; I'm hoping you are still seated, nodding, hands in your lap (with your eyes opened now...thank you very much...). I know, I know, I distracted you; I'm sorry. Take a minute and get back to that fluid motion. Once you have gotten that motion smoothed out, choose one or both of your hands (if you happen to be so fortunate), and while your head is moving in

23

a downward motion, swiftly bring the palms of your hands to your forehead to create a slapping sound.

(I really would be curious to learn how many people actually followed these ridiculous instructions that led them to even consider completing the task and thereby committing an act of self-harm, innocuous as it may be. I mean, there's got to be at least one...)

I also wonder how many of you tried, really tried, to get that motion to smooth out and just couldn't seem to get it to a natural feel. That is probably because I gave you the impression that I may have stumbled onto something that was going to help you like it helped me. Did you think I was about to teach you something? The reason that motion could not be achieved is because it is NOT a natural movement, not elliptical in any fashion. I lied to you from the start. So, if you believed the first lie, the rest came easy. Or did you choose not to worry about the truth and just go with the flow to see what happens? I know what you're thinking now: okay, this IS about to get political. No, again, what I just did has nothing to do with politics and everything to do with conditioning.

(uh-oh...maybe it is a little about politics...) We may come back to this but for now...

So, ...there I was, in my house, in "that" room, sitting at my desk, fingers poised over my keyboard as if I were going to stab the words into submission on the page. I have every intention of writing something uplifting. (...yeah...uplifting...) I sat and looked around the room.

Directly in front of me is my keyboard, two lovely monitors and some small speakers set just behind them. There is also an array of scribbled notes, bills to be paid, my phone, nail clippers, a few books covered up with some papers, a capo, a wallet and some more papers. There was a coffee cup from hours ago when I stormed away from my computer, not knowing anything about writing at the moment, or so I thought. Also on the desk are two random attachments for a hand-held vacuum cleaner that I have not used in weeks. There is a box of smaller boxes that contain the smaller attachments for phones and other chargeable devices, Tarot cards, tax papers to file, a sage stick, a lighter, a candle, a

24

couple of random oils, and my pre-filled out lottery tickets. (...somebody has to win, right? Why not me...) All of these things are within reach as I sit in my chair, centered on my desk. So, that is most of the stuff on this one level of my desk, but this desk has two more shelves in front of me. There are a couple of dozen books on the second shelf, not half of which I have even started to read.

me... *be honest, closer to two-thirds, not a half...*

also, me... *fine, but of that remaining third, I have finished reading about half of those... granted it has been so long that they should likely be read again...*

So, I have a collection of spiritually centered, self-awareness, self-help kind of publications. It is clear to me now that in order for these tools to be helpful, they must be used, in this case, read. Still on the second shelf, a change jar, two pencil jars, a small metal tongue drum, some crystals, some more candles, checkbooks, a stapler, a pencil sharpener, a guitar tuner, two zero response studio speakers, a tin of guitar picks. Third shelf: random handmade pottery, drumsticks, selfie sticks, a bowl of feathers, some more sage, a box of rocks, an alcohol lamp and spare reading glasses. So there you have it, and I have not even turned my head yet. I've been facing due south since I started writing. So when I tell you that my life is cluttered with things that prevent me from being who I feel I am at my core, I'm not bull-shittin'. Of all the things I mentioned above, very few are tools and information that have actually been used for their intended purpose....sad.

As I turn to the west, I see multiple guitars, some in need of re-stringing (all in need, and deserving of more use), a ukelele, a mandolin, various musical cordage and straps, a printer, turn table, two DAW's for recording music, various personal electronics (phones, chargers, power packs for medical devices, two crappy file cabinets (one actually organized), a practice speaker, a sketchbook (unused), a sleeping cat and my computer tower.

The north wall is frightening. It contains 4 small amplifiers (not used often enough), mic stands, picture frames, two cheesy shelves with boxed items such as two boxes of medical supplies, literature on essential oils, a box of various bottles for oils, tapes and CDs about health and fitness, stacking file separators with un-organized paperwork, a stack of hats and caps, and a 6' folding table covered in boxes being used to separate things for give away, for sale, for moving to other locations in the house and for trash.

The east wall has one closet filled with guitar cases, boxed supplements and oils, and an art folder with work that dates back forty years. There are two containers of family memorabilia and two boxes of secondhand devices for live and recorded music. There is a floor-to-ceiling bookcase filled with boxes containing microphones, guitar paraphernalia, pre-recorded music by others, blank disks for recording, songbooks, chord books, notebooks, stationary, some older studio interface equipment, computer cords and cables – much of it probably old tech to discard, another change jar, another box of rocks, an easel-art box, a Cajon and a vertical hanging shoe organizer for musical cables, cords, adapters, tuners, exercise bands, a few articles that were purchased stupid cheap intended for resale and potential profit, and finally assorted small things that have no other home.

All in all, I would surmise that at least half of what is in this room now shouldn't even be in this room.

__Me__… so what are you going to do about it?

__also me__… I think you mean us, don't you?

__me__… No, I mean you, the procrastinator….

--- and…..scene ---

…THE REAL WORLD re-enters my space (neighbor knocking and the phone call I ignored earlier, and I need to pee), which effectively HALTS the writing in real-time….

Three days later; So, I went back to read what I had written.

Where the hell was I going with this? It sounded as if I was about to start a fight with myself. Oh yes, now I remember. The whole thing was intended to be about the internal fight to stay present, to create, to connect with the unseen world around me. And how the seen world around us, coupled with our desire to live in known, predictable scenarios, steals the freedom that the spirit seeks beyond the mind and body. My comfort zone has become a cage filled with things and stuff that the analytical brain has deemed needed to help me create. Well, there's that, and there's the natural packrat in me that has yet to be tamed. I have been aware of this battle for some time now. I have written about it several times and have not yet found my way out. Perhaps this exercise is the one that sinks in and finally convinces me that enough is enough. I guess we'll see what I'm writing about a month or a year from now.

So, now I'll let you in on a little secret, I still have only a limited idea as to what I'm doing. I thought that "stream-of-consciousness writing" and "writing in real time" were the same thing. Well, they are not. My exercise in real-time writing was just letting my imagination run naked through my mind and I was typing as fast as I could to keep up, which is probably why the exercise sounds a little on the schizophrenic side of things. It is something I will likely never do again. Stream-of-consciousness writing is indeed pretty much everything else I write already, and I was unaware.

I regret to admit that more than three years from when I wrote The Marvelous Procrastinator is when I discovered "my format" for this book. That being said, sadly, most of the clutter is still in that room, but now, daily, I remove or discard at least one or two things. At this rate I may finish cleaning this room about the same time I finish writing this book. Since I have indeed written a few things dealing with clutter and procrastination in the past, I'll likely revisit this topic again later on. And by the way, I think "terrible" was probably the proper adjective after all.

(FYI, I googled "writing in real time" and was dumbfounded by the results. There are actually people who just make videos of themselves typing away on their laptops....and they have thousands of followers…W-T-F.)

...WALK WITH ME...

Until recently, I was pretty much a homebody. I left the house for work, ate lunch out, and stuff like that. But for multiple reasons, other than that, I got out very little. As I have grown older, I have seen in others that seclusion is in no way a healthy option for living. It became obvious this self-imposed lack of exposure and fellowship was going to be problematic, especially for someone who fancies themselves as a singer/songwriter. So, I started to make myself go out at least once a week. It was not always about music; sometimes, it was just for a long walk or a bite to eat, sometimes alone, sometimes with a friend.

Very shortly, this once-a-week outing made it painfully obvious that I needed to expand my comfort zone in a BIG way or do away with the "zone" concept completely. So, I started doing just that. I started sitting in on a coffee klatch comprised of local elder musicians and event organizers, some of whom I only knew by way of social media. (I was invited to attend by way of one thinly veiled, shared contact, whom I have not seen at any of the breakfasts I've attended so far) So, basically, I just showed up one day to have breakfast with a bunch of guys who didn't know I existed unless they just happened across me on Facebook or something. So, there I sat with relative strangers, hoping to glean some information or inspiration as they spoke of their years in "the music biz." I was taking mental notes. I found myself more interested in what did NOT work for them than what did. But I digress...

Last night, I went to a songwriter's circle at a local music listening room. The music scene in my town is interesting but, as of now, not what you would call....fresh. I saw a few folks there that I had met before over the years. I could not really call them friends. Most of them are only social media acquaintances. I mean, we never hung out together but occasionally attended the same musically oriented gatherings. There is a handful that I have had a few casual conversations with, but we have never collaborated, vented or otherwise shared any of our personal lives with each other.

When the show ended, the musicians and the audience began to mingle with one another. I hung around to say hello to a couple of those acquaintances I mentioned. Then I saw Linda. She was one of the handful that I had actually shared real time with a couple of years ago; she impressed me as an honest soul. When she performed, she sang from the heart, and you didn't just hear her; you felt her. She had been living out of town for a while but was now back. I made my way to her, and we hugged before saying a word. We chatted for about 5 minutes (mostly about me, I'm afraid); as we parted ways, we both reached out for another hug. It lasted for a period of time most folks would find uncomfortable. But I felt that honest soul again, as though we were hugging from the inside and not just clutching from the outside. I needed that. I did not realize how much I needed that.

It felt like kindred spirits, as though we were members of the same tribe. That soulful hug made me realize I was going to have to find more tribe. It also made me realize that I would like to have a lot more hugging in my life. What follows is sort of a poetic invitation to others who may be searching for the same type of closeness in their lives.

Walk with Me *(09/2018)*

If you want the rest of this story ... then take a walk with me....
I know nothing certain other than where I want to be
If your heart resonates with mine, then there is much to see
I'm ill-equipped to lead, but if you want to.... you can walk with me

If you want to know my deepest secrets... then take a walk with me....
If you listen as we wander, you'll hear more than you can see
Put your ego on a tether and embrace the mystery
I've no certifiable insights....but you can walk with me

If you see peace in all that is unspoiled...then take a walk with me
If the force of nature runs through your veins, rejoice and let it be
Sometimes, the body understands what the mind cannot conceive
And while you may think me too far out, if you want, you can walk with me

If confusion does not frighten you...then take this walk with me....
We'll dance on the penumbra, where the dark and light will meet
While heaven fills my head and Hades grapples at my feet
No one said this would be comfortable...but you can walk with me

If you're sated by the status quo....then please...don't walk with me...
Instead, go find a place to sit beneath an elder tree

31

Raise your face up to the filtered light, dig your toes down in the earth and see...

If you find no peace or solace there.... then please...don't walk me...

But if by chance you feel the power that brought us all upon this earth, and if even for a moment, you felt that love and felt its worth.

Then you'll understand how my words fail,

to capture the magic, to pull back the veil.

And while I'm still ill-equipped to lead anyone,

And I know my path is not the only one,

And I don't think this journey will ever be done,

If you care to, you can walk with me...

It would appear now that once I had decided to truly open myself up to others and do my best to expand my comfort zone, the universe said, " Okay, little mister....try this..." In the days that followed the afore-mentioned night of music, some of the people that I was in touch with musically years ago have re-surfaced. A few of the folks that I saw as only digital acquaintances have been reaching out to me. A brand-new batch of inspirations and what-ifs have been set before me to contemplate and take some sort of action on. I think that once I make the space for them, there will be many more collaborations in my future.

Hey, Linda... let's get dinner and talk...

...A PERSONAL DAY OFF...

I had a discussion last night with a friend who also writes. He mentioned how often his ideas come through as fragments, occasionally almost alien to one another. That conversation reminded me of something I wrote a couple of years ago. Once again, the battle between the hemispheres of the brain sparked a thought, and I allowed my artist self to run with it.

Dear God, sometimes I feel like I am so full of myself...

The fact of the matter is, my brain often goes off on little jaunts of its own—without me sometimes. It doesn't care where I am or what I'm doing. And I think if I don't try to document it in some way, it will just stay in my mind, getting tossed about, mixed in with other thoughts, fermenting and growing like a yeast roll. That could be dangerous for us all. Or, it could find a crack in the fence, get out, and run amok until I no longer remember where the thought started.

A Personal Day Off   *(09/2020)*

I took one of those recently—a personal day off. Not sick, no business to attend to, no pressing family obligations—just a day off. I spent some time trying to get my home office/studio into working readiness and re-reading things I've written. You know, poems, unfinished songs, bloggy notions. Turns out, a great many of these things I've written under the guise of insight or positivity are, in reality, passive-aggressive bitching. I write something almost every day, mostly because I can't not do so. On occasion, it's insightful, but all of it—by accident or by design—is a release for the emotional steam that gathers when exposed to everyday life, the news, work, personal well-being, and issues that other people's lives foist upon me. I also noticed that I get distracted very easily. I'm sixty-something years old with a forty-year-old attitude and a fervent wish for a thirty-year-old libido. All of that taken into account only means that it appears, even at this age, I still need a mentor, a guide, a handler—somebody or something to keep mashing the button on my shock collar every time I shout, "SQUIRREL."

I'm more anxious than ever for new challenges and victories—even small victories. I've determined that my biggest resentment about growing older isn't the things I didn't do; it's the things I still must do to survive. The things that rob my energy and my time from the here and now, and the things I want to do the most. It's a cycle that I hope will eventually break itself.

But for now, it's like an awkward square dance where the conscious mind and mortal limitations are coupled, and they're dancing across the square with the subconscious mind, which happens to be partnered with spiritual curiosity. Self-preservation is calling the dance, while the ego and the id are locked in a battle royale on the fiddle and the banjo. The speed of the dance, almost without notice, increases until it reaches a frenetic pace. The sound of clogging feet grows louder and louder as the dance speeds up. Then the caller shouts, "Ladies center, men sashay around the square...all change partners and promenade..." BANG!! Partners swap, and all hell breaks loose!

For what it's worth, I feel that most artists (again, it doesn't matter what kind) have some sort of ADD, ADHD, DID, psychosis, or neurosis at play in their little brains at some point in time. In other words, not quite right in the head. More often than not, it's not severe enough for the general public to recognize on any given day. But nonetheless, I think it's there. So, when I refer to a "personal" day off, it really is more like a mental health holiday. I don't care who you are, artist or not; we all need a mental health day from time to time.

Tell me I'm wrong...

...ANCIENT MENTORS...

As I've been compiling this book, I've begun to notice that many of the things I write focus on the search for that "voice" that lives within us all. You know it—I know you do—the voice that tries either to lead us in a certain direction or stop us in our tracks. Some would say it's our subconscious mind at work. Some would say it's our hubris or our guilt at play in our decision-making. But the more often I force myself to find time to be still, to quiet myself in meditation, the more I hear that voice. And the more I hear that voice, the more I'm convinced that the source of it is pure energy—energy that spins all around us, all of the time. And we are physical/metaphysical antennae, designed to receive those energies.

In my own life and my ongoing search for spiritual growth, I'll continue to find ways to train myself as a conductor for those energies. I believe there's a significant amount of residual energy to be found and felt in the land—in the rocks and trees themselves—that were present when our histories were made.

Those energies contain the past, the present, and perhaps the future too, to some extent. The energies in question are both positive and negative. They must exist together to maintain a spiritual balance. When I say positive and negative, it's not meant to imply good versus evil—not at all. What follows is another stream of thoughts that represents both energies, as both are required to create.

Ancient Mentors   *(11/2018)*

Ancient mentors, foreign tongues, chastise me for works undone

I do not hear the words, but I feel them all the same

The prophets and the sages, who once reached out from cages

Now beg of me to free my mind and pen the empty pages

Of the history that lies unwritten still, of those who dared to stand alone in peace upon a hill,

the artists, teachers, healers, steadfast in their wills,

with a light so overwhelming that the darkness becomes filled.

The infancy of our human past was survival first and compassion last

our clans, our tribes, still little more than herds

Then someone began to understand abundance grew from helping hands

And weapons might be needed less when connected by our words

Ah, but instincts of survival always lay in wait as rivals,

and along with wielding weapons, they grow greed

Greed questions all contentment by offering resentment and helping to confuse our wants with needs

Our separate civilizations grew a myriad of nations and too a greater space between the rich and those in rags

Our loyalty to humanity is still locked in our geography, still nothing more than larger clans with flags.

On and off throughout time were the questioning minds found in dungeons or banished afar,

*Labeled heretics, witches, insane sons of bitches who would dare
to challenge the way that things are.*

*You see, I believe in the wisdom of elders, the spiritual knowledge
of bygone days,*

*I believe, like a river, it still flows above us amid the din of our
progress, obscured by toxic haze.*

I want to know their secrets, and if I must, I'll feel their pain

If that's what it takes to find the purity in humanity once again

*So here I am now, a sleepless romantic with an urge to create that
borders on manic.*

*I work to survive, but I don't feel alive... and I'm considering
drugs for my panic.*

You see, the details of my working life sometimes follow me to bed

*and ensure that when I wake too soon, they will be there in my
head*

What I feel sometimes beneath it all defies an explanation,

*Sometimes, I think I've lost my mind and that the train has left the
station*

*Even daydreams now begin to fade, those spaces filled with things
undone,*

*I'm pretty sure this is unacceptable; my muse is screaming,
"RUN!".*

So, I am writing this at four a.m., forcing thoughts upon a page,

with hopes of finding peace within to counter all this rage

I sit at my computer, just staring at the screen,

I'm hoping to be brilliant, whatever the hell that means

I want to choose words wisely; I want them to convey

the spirit of the moment once my muse has had her way

I know it's there…as it always is….just waiting patiently,

for me to peel back the madness and finally set it free

Sometimes, a whispered warning says your doubt will get the best of you

If you spend your time regretting all the things you did not do

So choose what is important now, pack away the rest and lose the bags

Don't let your ability to share yourself be reduced to emojis and tags

I know there's more to communication than carefully chosen phrases

Sometimes, it's the silence between the lines and the expressions on your faces

Take the time, find the words to express yourself,

but do it with this in mind

We're here because of ALL the love that ever was,

all of it has been multiplied

All things have a vibration, and they are meant to harmonize,

Stretch your hands up with mine to the river of ages, open your heart and close your eyes

Let the river then run through us, and let's see what it leaves behind,

Perhaps a sediment of sentiment that we'll be hard-pressed to describe.

What should we glean from history, if not the lessons to be learned

To save ourselves from needless wars, peoples, cities, and nations burned

So now I sit here in this cyclone, try to focus on the thinking

I write because I cannot not, and I sound like I've been drinking

I suppose that what I'm trying to say is that I believe a better world is reachable.

That fighting the madness is not madness, and certainly, all are teachable

Let love shed new light on hatred; let peace be the sails to our boat

Can we agree that our past is a warning and not to be repeated in rote

Ancient mentors, foreign tongues, chastise me for works undone

I do not hear the words, but I feel them all the same.

The prophets and the sages, who once reached out from cages,

Now beg of me to free my mind and pen the empty pages,

Of the history that lies unwritten still, of those who dare to stand alone in peace upon a hill,

the artists, and teachers, and healers, steadfast in their wills,

with a light so overwhelming that the darkness becomes filled.

So, this poem you just read is another example of a message trying to get through. For me, one of the truths I've adopted—and which I believe is undeniable—is that when it comes to our histories, we must all remember our past. The uplifting parts, the shameful parts, the soulful and soulless parts all have lessons to teach. I was shocked to learn that in some schools around the country, history courses don't include any mention of the

Holocaust during World War II. How can this be? In fact, many of the darker portions of history are being swept under the rug. Why?

I encourage you to get a little angry about this. If we allow the ugly parts of our past to be erased from our children's education, then the lessons to be learned from that painful history will also vanish. I don't recall where I heard it, but I once read an addendum to a famous quote about this subject…. The original quote (George Santayana), "Those who cannot remember the past are condemned to repeat it," …then this, those who willfully erase the past are the ones ensuring our condemnation to that fate.

...KEEP ON TALKING...

Lately, (here at the beginning of a new election cycle) I've been feeling a push to be more philosophical/political. (...as if you couldn't already tell...) But not being one of those individuals who immerses themselves in reading or listening to political pundits leaves me with little to back up my views other than my gut reactions or my intuition about the things I do read, or see or hear. Recently, the air seems filled with discontent. The season is upon us when we, the people, will soon be given the opportunity to vote for those we hope will lead us. I haven't been happy with the choices presented to me for some time, yet I don't feel disheartened. I still believe there's a growing sentiment that supports a kinder, gentler government. But when others speak to me as if I'm ignorant or performing a disservice to my country by NOT allowing myself to be overwhelmed with political rhetoric, I can't help but feel defensive. Still, I really try hard not to.

I've realized that in regular conversations with someone who does not—or will not—keep an open mind, there's little hope for any true exchange of information or feelings. I know that might sound like I've given up on meeting someone halfway. But it's probably more accurate to say that I'm just tired of spending so much time filtering through the lies and misdirection in the game of politics. By the literal definition of the word "politician," it means one who practices the science and art of politics, usually with respect to a particular party's agenda. So I say let's get politicians out of government and bring in more representatives.

Keep on Talking   *(02/2016)*

(or, Fuck Around and Find Out)

Just because you do not know me, that doesn't mean I can't be trusted

If you're choosing to be cautious, that's just fine

But if you're choosing to be filled with hate as if there were no option

Understand that it is a poisoning of the mind

I understand this world is not my own; I'm just a steward of its care

Yet most with the means to make a change often seem so unaware

I don't begrudge your wealth at all, yet you begrudge my need

And the valley of the middle ground grows deeper thanks to greed

   But keep on talking down to me like I don't understand,

   Go on believing you can't be anything but right.

   Keep on blaming me for losing because you hold a better hand.

   And you can hate me if that helps you sleep at night.

You've told me I have freedom; you've told me I have a chance

But you limit me by your decrees, and you stymie all my plans

We, the working poor, just living week to week

With no change in our pockets, with ends.....that rarely meet

Too wealthy for assistance, too broke to fix my car

42

Insurance I can't afford to use,.......and that's just how things are?

The gaps are planned and tailored to keep me where I am

A debt-based life is the future of the average working man

But keep on talking down to me, like I can't understand,

Go on believing that your power makes you right.

Your disdain becomes a blindfold that, when finally

ripped away

May cause you to be blinded by the light

So, as you take yourself to bed, remember I'm still here

I lay awake and hungry, and that should be your fear

When a man has next to nothing, then he's not afraid to lose

And if you've trapped him in the corner, there's but one path left to choose

Someday, like a prophecy fulfilled, the bitter ends will meet

By joining hands in peace or with fists out in the street

But a circle must be fashioned to protect us, every one

Or this earth will see us vanquished in the shame of what's undone

So, keep on talking down to me like I won't understand,

But be wary if you challenge me to fight.

In time, all of your conscripts will finally see the truth

And that truth is what helps me sleep at night.

I know… it sounds a bit like a threat, right? Well, sometimes, a warning can feel like that. And if someone feels that the warning has singled them out, then that should be a pretty clear sign that the warning was indeed meant for them.

For some, this might be preaching to the choir. For others, perhaps, it's a cold slap in the face to jar them out of whatever trance they've been operating from. Now, my opinions are my own, but I've said it before—and I'm sure I'll say it again—most of my poetic or musical thoughts seem to come *through* me, not *from* me. I usually have very little time to document my basic thoughts. Then it sort of becomes a puzzle, and I must try to fill in the missing parts while still making sense somehow. I've accepted that I don't get to change the channel on this cosmic boob tube. I rather like this channel, but if you don't care for it, you don't have to watch.

...CAME TO PASS...

Now, I do not want to leave you thinking that I am bitter about such things because I am not. In fact, I continue to be ever hopeful that society will have little choice but to change once it sees where a negatively aggressive posture will take it. I am praying that we have this epiphany before we reach a point of no return—and there usually is such a thing as a point of no return. History tells us of many civilizations that flourished and then failed. Because I have written many times on the subject, I will follow up with another piece I wrote in 2018. The election cycle was two years away at the time, yet voices were already being raised in discontent.

I felt I saw a greater movement than what was being reflected in regular media formats. In some venues, more than just politics was being discussed. A growing discussion emerged—not about left- or right-leaning politics, but the morals of this country. And no, I am not talking about religion. The most basic moral behaviors were finding their way back into debates on social inequities. People were beginning to talk about the battle for the soul of this nation, as though it might actually have one that could be lost.

Came to Pass   *(09/2020)*

... And then there came to pass a gentle rustling sound, like leaves being blown about by the wind, this way and that—a gentle rustling that grows more intense with each passing day... can you hear it yet?

The sound is, in part, from America's heartland walking out of town hall meetings, disgruntled by the evasiveness or silence of those being questioned.

The sound is, in part, coming from the youngest citizens as they begin to march in the streets, seeking truth and justice for the first time.

The sound is, in part, coming from the oldest citizens, beginning to march into the halls of government, demanding what they have earned with their bodies, their time, and their dedication—seeking fulfillment of the promises this country once offered as a reward for their participation.

The sound is, in part, coming from veterans who, by choice or by law, have given their all in service to the country, only to realize— more often than not—they unknowingly supported some uncaring financial power behind the government's actions. Now their government does not go out of its way to help them in return.

The sound is, in part, a byproduct of the shuffling of feet in the pews at the rear of the church, as crestfallen members of the congregation tuck their faith back into their Bibles and leave, one by one—no longer edified by the words of false prophets behind the pulpits who bid them to believe in the abilities of self-proclaimed saviors.

Louder grows the sound of the righteously indignant as truly honest men and women see the lies and refuse the compromises struck in their name behind closed doors.

Faster grows the exodus from a place of hollow promises as the subterfuge is uncovered—the very makers of the mayhem now scrambling for their lives, hastily packing up what they can fit in their carpetbags and abandoning a once-promising republic to be shredded by a country they intentionally divided.

We, the lost, forgotten souls, grow weary of waiting, our futures in more peril than ever before. Those who swore to us in public to help with our burdens were given our light, in trust, to carry. Many have carried that light with them into private chambers, where loyalty becomes a commodity and is always up for sale. Their secretive endeavors leave us in darkness, wondering, praying, arguing amongst ourselves—mostly ignorant of their actions until some blatant scandal is uncovered. And when the wealthy subversives are caught, rarely is the sentence harsh. Rarely does the penance levied in any way help correct the damages done.

A change is going to come. I pray for the words to write and sing, words that touch hearts hardened by lies. Oh, to find the words that act as antidotes to the poison creating the growing disappointment and selfishness looming over us—its weight increasing with every angry word and deed. I pray for the words to write and sing, words to ignite fires in hearts longing for light so they may see their own path to that place where peace and love are the rule, not the exception.

Do you want to heal hearts, to bridge the chasm growing wider with every furrowed brow and wagging finger? Can you help me find the words? If you can, and if you dare, speak them, write them, sing them, scream them, etch them in stone—and use those stones to help create a new foundation for future citizens to stand upon, build upon, take pride in, and share freely the benefits of true cooperation with one another. It is time to proclaim, with an inclusive heart and soul, that phrases like "...Liberty and Justice for all" are not just words but a badge of honor we wear into battle—a guidepost in every reaction to injustice, foreign and domestic. Let's fight together again, for the first time, as we each wage our own internal war, striving to be better spirits inside these human suits we wear. We must remember that light was born out of darkness. So, too, can we be lights born out of the darkness. We can and should help hold each other up into the light.

Hallelujah, Brothers and Sisters, lift your voices to the sky and sing it with me…! This little light of mine, I'm going to let it shine…

…C'mon… you know this one, or at least you used to…

I'm putting away my soap box for a bit now...

...THE CANDY JAR...

...Okay... brace yourselves... In recent weeks, I have been completely preoccupied with sex. I suppose it's more accurate to say *the absence thereof.* Even before I became a widower, that part of my life was not exactly all I'd hoped for. There were, of course, quite understandable reasons for this, but I need not tell you too much about my private life. Regardless of the reasons, however, my mental gymnastics on the subject rarely took a break.

So now, for the last couple of months, that mental fracas has been a major distraction from all the other topics I wish to write about. It's said the stereotypical male supposedly thinks about sex in some fashion about twenty or so times a day, women about ten. Well, today, I got to thinking about *how* I think of women. Granted, there are those thoughts that are strictly for a moment's pleasure, *but* moreover, I find myself having fantasies that are really more about the mystique of a woman. I find myself thinking less about what I would want to do *to* her and more about what she might reveal of herself to me should she desire me enough.

Literature is littered with sex and/or the desire for sex. I've written a few truly X-rated pieces of fluff. But I've also tried to capture the beauty and the frustration of the search for that moment when she decides to become *supplicant* to her lover.

The Candy Jar *(05/5/21)*

I do not know now when it began or if, in fact, it always was and has just never ended. As fire tempers steel, so too can the fire itself often be tempered, altered by time. Skin grows thinner, minds grow more cluttered with everyday needs, and wants become liken to a candy jar upon a high shelf, always in view, providing temptation...daily.

Why do I never grow bold enough to just take the jar at my whim?

Why does the jar not come to me? Surely, by now, it knows of my intention to possess it.

Shall I climb the shelves, hoping they will hold the weight of my desires?

Is it folly to be so enraptured, dare I risk the fall?

In my mind the effort is rewarded, even if not truly earned.

And in that fantasy, where my will propels me into action, I do indeed reach that shelf and the jar upon it.

I now imagine dipping my fingers into the sweet offering, and I am most assuredly made dumb with glee.

While I had it in my grasp I could greedily, selfishly take it all, leaving only a void inside the jar.

But the reality is that which remains in the jar, the seen and yet unknown, is what feeds my desire.

That which is not had becomes the quest once again.

In my boyish dreams, the jar gives itself to me with no regard for my deserving.

It gives itself to me because it, too, finds a type of pleasure there.

It gives itself to me so that I am always able to taste it still upon my tongue.

But the jar has its own frailties, and the beautiful glass can be broken if I am careless in my handling of it.

I find myself next to the jar but dare not risk clumsily knocking it off its shelf in my growing anticipation to claim it as my very own.

So close and yet still unsure of my abilities to balance the beautifully fragile jar and the delicacies within as I carry the jar down to meet me.

If the air itself around the jar could be enough to sate my desire, I would simply wade into the wafting aroma and bathe myself in the thrill of it all.

But the air offers no comfort, and the climb promises no reward.

The air offers only a whiff of scent to remind me of the flavors I have known before.

Deliciously cruel are the memories of sweet delights from jars now void of even recollection of their spell.

The air unknowingly mocks me and reminds me that as much as I will never stop wanting it, it does not share those same desires.

And as much as I might want to, as deeply as I desire to learn the secrets of the untested pleasures, it will likely remain in a dream.

And sadly, I will likely never know what it must be like to be such a jar.

When I think about it, I was very fortunate that, for the majority of my forty-eight years of marriage, love, lust, and sex were nicely combined with one another. I always felt lucky to have a woman who understood that I enjoyed her pleasure almost as much as my own. And for many years, I was blessed again that the reverse was just as true. For me, experiencing the quest for that enjoyment was just as important as the enjoyment itself.

Sadly, as time marched forward, my dogs grew weary in my well-worn boots, my arches fell, and my varicose veins began to look like a road map. I had adopted a lackadaisical attitude toward writing or speaking in words that could be titillating. I had become a guy who stood little chance of having his face slapped for overstepping boundaries. I mean, I never had the desire to be a pig or so forward as to be considered creepy. But that sometimes-questionable side of my personality was slipping away. My shoes became more sensible, my manner of dress a bit too casual, and my own passions started to feel like a film you've watched too many times to be considered a healthy habit.

But in writing this book, while I went back to review old poems and stories from bygone years, I started to remember what those passions felt like. As if recovering from temporary amnesia, those little memories began to light small fires. Before long, as the embers started to glow a little brighter, I decided to start fanning the flames again. There was a lot of joy in those older, intimate, carnal moments.

Now... I just need some wood to keep things going...

Let me rephrase that, now I just need someone who can be fuel to the fire.

...THE BIRDS AND SOME BE'S...

Can you identify with the metaphoric prose in The Candy Jar? Assuming that you still entertain carnal desires, are you one of the people who sees a spiritual connection with regard to desire and the act of sex? Or are you one of those who sees the physical act of sex as totally independent of the spiritual self? I suppose that my feelings on the matter are largely due to the fact that I was raised in a home with a couple (my parents, in case you had not figured that out yet...) that honored the "till death do you part" vow. While growing up, I did not really see them as sexual beings. There were precious few public displays of affection, but honor and cherish were indeed plain to see. It wasn't until I was married with kids that I began to truly understand the challenges of such a commitment.

Now my kids saw plenty of affection being shared in our household. I could not keep my hands off my wife. And for almost all of our time together, she found it uplifting and still desired to be touched. Tons of hugging and kissing, and the words "I love you" were heard many times a day, not only between us but with our kids as well... in a non-sexual context, thank you very much...

I always saw her as desirable. I was always able to see the girl I fell in love with inside the woman she became, aging right along with me. I know I am one of the luckiest few in that she and I had an instant connection, practically electrical, from our very first kiss. Perhaps that is what made me certain that there IS a spiritual connection, even in the libertine nature of having sex just for the sake of having sex. When my kids started wondering about sex and such matters, the only advice I gave them was that in my opinion... anytime you do have sex with someone, there is an exchange of energies. You are sharing a piece of yourself that you do not get to retrieve. That is where the heart and soul come into play. You should feel certain that this person you are sharing with is capable of sharing in return and can be trusted to cherish that part of yourself that you are leaving with them."

Especially for teens, helping them understand the concept of trust in an intimate relationship is very important. I know many adults who still carry emotional scars because someone they thought loved them really saw them as nothing more than a conquest. After the fact, they were ghosted, or worse yet, made a spectacle of in social circles. And now, today, with the seemingly endless variety of social media, that kind of humiliation can be so much worse.

Any of you who might be reading this, please take my advice: do not pull your punches when discussing such things with your own children or younger siblings. It is far better to embarrass them yourself now instead of having it happen within their peer group. You are an adult, maybe even a grown-up, and they probably already resent you for some stupid stuff anyhow. But later, they will thank you for your blatant honesty and caring. Unless, of course, they are just assholes by nature… and hopefully, they will grow beyond that too.

All of that being said, now a widower, I still hope to find an attractive, kindred spirit who understands and agrees with my fauxlosophy on the matter and would still like to bump uglies while she can, which brings us to part two of this uncomfortable offering. To hopefully complete the thoughts, here is my view on being in an ALL IN in a relationship…

The Birds and Some Be's   *(12/2020)*

does reality ever compare to fantasy…

do passionate dreams enthrall us because they are rooted in the subconscious memory or because they allow a boundless imagination and a limitless invitation to fulfill our desires with no hesitation, with no fear of judgment, with no fear of shame?

the truth is that fantasy pales by default to a reality where lovers not only allow but extend the limitless invitation to their partners and themselves. perfect imperfections retreat, and the mind sees only that which is longing to be seen, in all of its purity and in its irreverence.

be the leader, be the follower, be the victor, be the vanquished,

be the giver, be the taker, be the seducer, be the seduced,

be caring, be careless, be gentle, be rough, be the actor, be the director, be coy, be blunt,

be silent, be loud, be ever so serious, be breathless from laughter, be timid, be unafraid, be yourself, be somebody else,

be in love, be in lust, be reliably comfortable, be surprisingly wicked,

be spiritual nourishment, be the dessert, be the smile, be the reason the smile exists and lingers….

Have you had any thoughts on the matter? Can you accept the contradictions? Can you see the contrary nature of love versus lust? I'd be willing to bet somebody would be interested in your perspective on this conundrum… Maybe even your significant other, if you have yet to open up to them. My opinion: it is better to be disliked for who you are than to be liked for someone you are not.

...I LOVE YOU ANYWAY...

On this particular day, I got up with no real plan for my day. I was expecting a visit from a middle management person from a roofing company I was currently at odds with. BUT... that has very little to do with the underlying energies I have been experiencing for the last few days. In general, I have been noticing in my and others' lives that we are making attempts to uncover and separate our past hurts and disappointments from where we live in the here and now. Along with that must come the intention for self-protection from those energies and their origins once we name them and cast them away. On the surface, that sounds simple, but it does take a certain amount of determination, and we must remind ourselves of those intentions if those negative energies try to outflank us later on.

Along with that, if we are to see any real gain from the above-mentioned intentions, comes the need for us to express forgiveness to others who may have been responsible (even if only partly responsible) for those pains. That is not the same as forgetting... that is where the "protection" comes in. And while we are forgiving others for their roles in our traumas or disappointments, we must find the means by which to forgive ourselves for our roles therein as well. It always hurts a little to inspect your own faults and the guilt that may be hovering about them.

While thinking about all of the above, I was searching through older, unfinished poetry and music when I found a song that had quite literally been kicked around for a decade. I know, procrastinate much? Anyway, I had never found the groove for this song until today. I remembered a little of the original melody and fumbled my way through the chorus while playing my guitar. I instantly found problems with the cadence of the lyrics. These issues could only be fixed by altering the words somewhere. As I began to play with that, I became aware of "mixed messages" within the storyline of the song itself.

It is a love song, and while it did express a desire to love this person, pleading, in fact, to allow it, it also had moments where it placed blame on the same person for their difficulties in developing the relationship. It occurred to me that it was okay to name the problems, but not at all okay (for me/us/third parties) to blame this person for their difficulties. **Sometimes, the past is a very hard thing to let go of. After all, everything we are now was created by our past. The subject in this song has to relinquish himself and his desire to "fix" this woman. Even though he knows that she is having a hard time allowing herself to let the past be the past, he can do nothing but offer love and patience. He is accepting the frustration of loving her even if, in the long run, it cannot be fully reciprocated.

I Love You Anyway   *(06/2015)*

Girl, I thought you might find some peace,

Here inside the love I'm trying to share.

You've gotten used to running to protect your heart.

And all my friends keep telling me,

There ain't the future that I'd like to see.

But I keep on believing, I have right from the start.

I love you anyway,

I love you anyway,

There ain't no doubt you turn me inside out,

But I love you anyway.

Take my hand and trust me, baby,

Give yourself a chance to see.

I can show more of love than you ever thought could be.

Let your past be lessons learned,

But not a wall where we're concerned

Try to free your mind, babe, and fall in love with me.

I love you anyway,

I love you anyway,

There ain't no doubt you turn me inside out,

But I love you anyway.

Girl, I wish that you could understand,

Just how much you mean to me.

And I think I know you better than you might believe.

I am sure I can never know

The depth of pain you feel,

I understand your heart has been broken, but why you won't let it heal?

I love you anyway,

I love you anyway,

There ain't no doubt you turn me inside out,

But I love you anyway.

> *I'm gonna love you anyway.*
> *Let me love you anyway*
> *I love you anyway....*

I must be on to something, you guys. As I was writing this installation with its discussion on pain, forgiveness, self-protection, and such, a friend contacted me and interrupted me to share what was happening with him, here and now. Up above where the double asterisk is, yeah, there, that is when he called to tell me good news concerning himself and a woman he fell in love with about a year and a half ago. They met online (not a dating site, but yes, a long-distance relationship), and once they started writing and calling each other on a regular basis, their relationship grew quickly. He went to finally meet her in person, and it did not go well. They hit a wall hard when she could not get beyond her past traumas enough to clear the way for a new love. He tried to help her, but she wasn't ready to let go. He told her that until she got herself in order, they really couldn't go any further. He was miserable that he had to do so, but he had to do that to protect himself and his spirit. Well, she reached out to him a few days ago. She has been working on herself for a year, clearing away the debris from previous relationships, and it looks like they will once again begin conversing...

Also, while I was re-writing the lyrics to that song, I was multi-tasking and listening to a video blog from an Earth Magic Mama that I follow. She was talking about the sea salt she was reducing to use in her jewelry and selling for protection purposes. She explained that there was a recipe for creating it and gave instructions on how and what to use it for. It turned out that a large part of her video revolved around not only protecting one's spiritual self but also the power of forgiveness in the maintenance of one's spirit. She spoke of the importance of doing all things with love, saying that there was no practical use for anger or fear in setting protective boundaries. If you are placing protective intentions for yourself out of love for yourself, then the negative energies of anger, fear, or hate only diminish your own power.

...SPIN ART...

What a strange morning this has been. I do, on occasion, wake up feeling lonely, not desperately, mind you, but all the same, sometimes wishing there was a special someone with whom to cuddle or have a cup of coffee. Someone to talk with about dreams, the sleeping and the waking kind. After a very long marriage, you grow accustomed to that privilege and hopefully never lose sight of the fact that it is indeed a privilege. But since there was not that someone on this morning, my head began to cycle through a myriad of things and stuff concerning home repairs, finances, and other "worldly" bruhaha. I determined that writing might be a better use of my time. So, I crawled out of bed, put on a robe, started walking to the kitchen for coffee, tripped over the cat, and told him what a jerk he was… yadda-yadda-yadda, normal morning stuff. I got my coffee, sat at my computer, determined to write something to entreat the mind, and then… like I said, what a strange morning this has been.

It often happens that my train of thought jumps the tracks once in a while. It could be that undiagnosed artist's ADD I talked about earlier, or my advanced years are fuckin' around with my synaptic patterns. Either way, this morning has been extra special.

When you were a kid, did you ever have a model train set? Well, if you did, then you know how easily a derailment can happen. Too sharp a turn, too much speed, or a little piece of anything on the tracks themselves all have the same result. One or more cars will tip ever so slightly too far and fall right over, usually taking more cars with it. That is me this morning. I try to focus on a little something long enough to document it, and another little something comes along to derail it in mid-thought. Then I realize that along with this secondary thought, not only has my mind's eye been thwarted, but apparently my actual eyes, too! When I shake my brain to get back to the original thought, I notice my eyes are indeed closed. What the hell? Am I that sleep-deprived? Is there some other force at work that does not want me to THINK and share?

So, today, the mental train keeps derailing. Okay, so what? I've dealt with that before. All I need to do is set the train back on the tracks and keep going, only maybe a little slower. However, I told you this morning has been "special." This morning even the interruptions to my train of thought have interruptions, most of them vaguely relatable at best. Try to imagine that... if even your daydreams had daydreams.

Now imagine that our train set is set up on a very large table. It is a really nice one, too, with buildings and trees, little people doing whatever little plastic people do, a painted pond, and maybe even a tunnel. Anyway, while playing with my train today, not only has the train derailed many, many times, but today it has even fallen off the damned table a few times, and now some of the cars are chipped or cracked, the roof of the caboose came off, the engine's smokestack is bent, and the little engineer from inside it is nowhere to be found.

Yes, indeed, what a strange morning this has been.

Spin Art *(04/21)*

I have been blue with sadness.
I have been red with passion
I have been green with envy
A slave to emotional fashion

I have been golden when hopeful.
I've been brown when I was tired
I have been maudlin in jet black
I have been beige when uninspired

I've been yellow and cheerful.
I've been dainty in pink
I've been manic in purple
So what do you think?

Am I fearful of changes?
Am I hopelessly lost?
Am I Pollock on a bender
or the spirit of Bob Ross?

Am I a prophet in a blender,
am I a poet playing games?
Am I the player or the referee
in this existential game?

Am I a teacher or a student,
am I a child or fully grown?
Am I the rainstorm or the rainbow,
am I the frickin' Pot O' Gold?

Manic depressive, ...yeah...its possible,
psychotic , ...mmm...could be,
bi-polar, ... too much trouble,
for a person much like me

Sometimes, I'm in a stupor
Sometimes I can't shut up
Sometimes I see things clearly,
even through my daily muck

I like the unexpected
I like goofy and absurd
But what I LOVE is finger-painting,
making pictures with my words

Well, the day and my mind remained splintered, and about all I accomplished was a little housework and creating a spreadsheet where I could dump all my errant thoughts in writing... just notes, really. I hope I can develop the habit of remanding stuff to the spreadsheet and checking in on it from time to time so I can check things OFF the list, but only time will tell.

Suddenly, I feel like a social media personality who presents a show and tells about how cool their life is. And then one day, they have a little breakdown and post a video, crying, makeup running down their cheeks. Through the tears, they tell the whole world how stressful trying to be cool all the time actually is.

Thank God I don't have to worry about that. I have never tried to be anything but my real self, warts and all. I lay myself bare sometimes, keeping my heart on my sleeve. I don't think I have ever been cool, plus I only ever wear waterproof mascara, just in case.

...ROOMS AS OPPOSED TO ROOM...

Recently, I have felt like a visitor in my own home. There is nobody making me feel this way; it is just an energy that is currently in the air. I do not feel as if I am in danger. I do not feel as if anyone is deliberately trying to make me uncomfortable, yet I am. For the last few days, I have actually been quite motivated to read, meditate, and create. But I had to leave my house to take advantage of those energies.

After my wife passed, I was here alone for about a year and a half. It took every bit of that time to feel anywhere near normal again. I began a gentle purge and examination of this house and how to make it work for me now that it did not have to make space for anyone but me. I was going to set up two studios in my home: one as a writer's nook/music studio, the other for visual arts. I began the task of boxing, cleaning, re-arranging, and "letting go" of parts of a previous life to make way for a new chapter.

All of that came to an unexpected halt. Circumstances placed me in the position of becoming a safety net for one of my kids as their life came apart after a bad relationship. Everything I had begun to do had to be packed and stacked into two rooms I was living in to make room for two more people in my home. Do not misunderstand this; as much as I disliked the thought of unhappy and temporarily unemployed people living with me, I did, and I do feel grateful that I was in a position to do just that. I'm certain there is some repressed anger that I will have to deal with, but that is for another time.

Now, after nearly a year, it appears I will once again be here by myself. And perhaps being in a place where I once again have to re-evaluate what is important in my life. I am getting to a point in my life where what I own is directly related to what I can maintain. That is the reason that I have had to really look at myself and the clutter and confusion that has settled in around me over the years. Perhaps the physical purge will aid in the mental purge as well.

I wrote this in the first couple of months after my wife passed as I tried to determine what to do with my house. And three years later, here I am again…

…Rooms, as opposed to Room... *(05/21)*

(…finding the clutter that blocks the flow… part un)

Definition of room, according to Webster

1: an extent of space occupied by or sufficient or available for something <room to run and play>

2 obsolete: an appropriate or designated position, post, or station: place, stead <in whose room I am now assuming the pen — Sir Walter Scott>

3: a partitioned part of the inside of a building, especially such a part used as a lodging: the people in a room

4: a suitable or fit occasion or opportunity: chance <no room for doubt>

Today, I pondered the difference between a room and room, both literally and figuratively. I have both, but at times, both present me with the challenge of making decisions for their optimal use, which are confusing at best. These decisions, taken at face value, seem like simple enough choices that could be made with little or no contemplation… but… Not taking the time to think through the purpose of a room and the usage of its space can lead to it becoming a space that collects items at random and turns into a space that is confusing and lacks a spirit of its own.

So, what is a room? A room is a physically defined space with finite edges, with the limitations of three dimensions: height, width, and depth. Remember these dimensions for later. So, here we are with a defined space, and it is now time to determine what to do with that space. There are two very general categories regarding the usage of a room; these are best described as inclusion or exclusion. Will it be a place where anyone with a proper invitation can spend time? Or will it be a space set aside for private use? The things you keep in these rooms will be very different, all a part of who you are and what your space reflects, but still very different. You may have several rooms at your disposal, but all will follow the same two general usage rules. I do not wish to investigate or debate any particular take on what constitutes public or private usage; suffice it to say that there is entirely too much middle ground in such a discussion.

You can choose to decorate rooms sparsely, with very little furniture, very little décor, very little whimsy, very little color... very little character. Or you may choose to emblazon the walls in bright, daring colors and fill them up with shelves full of things, art, rugs, and oversized furniture until very little of the actual room can be seen. In a sense, decorating your room has as much to do with what you wish to show others about yourself as it does with showing parts of you to yourself that you wish to be reminded of.

Decorating a room becomes a balancing act of purposeful form, prioritized function, and pure fancy. The skill it takes to find that balance is an art all unto itself; my wife had that skill in spades. That skill is the remarkable difference between housekeeping and homemaking. A generic decorator may be able to mix and match colors and textures while blending vintage and modern styles, but cannot do what a homemaker does because they lack the personal knowledge and care needed to set a stage for a loved one's comfort physically, emotionally, and spiritually.

There is an actual room in my home where these current passages of thought were born. This room is the space that I wish to see become the launch pad to my life's second act. This place is where all of the thoughts presently trapped in my head get to leak out gently, flow out freely, or spew out uncontrollably. I have come to think of this "physical room" and the "room" in my head in much the same fashion. But the problem at hand for me now is that even the most gifted homemaker cannot help put either of these rooms into clear focus for this user. This balancing act is not really about beauty or comfort. The balance here is the often fine line between pragmatic function and theoretical form, the difference between having what you need and needing what you have. This line of demarcation is not always easily seen, mentally or physically, but for your own good, you must search for it, uncover it, or flat-out create it and stake claim to it.

There is a fantasy space where everything is at your fingertips, willing to do your bidding as if it were a pet awaiting your attention. Then there is the real space where almost everything you think you need is there but somehow is always just out of reach or hidden from view by some random item that you laid down on top of it the day before. This room of mine and its décor must help to both promote and protect inspiration. Tools must be easily accessible without being in the way, laid out simply enough to allow change without major modification, and a layout that will allow a shift in focus without the need for complicated rearranging.

In the case of a home studio/office/writer's nook, the coming and going of instruments, various musical accessories, computers, hardware, and software, not to mention the myriad of hand-scrawled notes on various mediums from legal pads to napkins, makes for a fair amount of confusion all by themselves. Sometimes, it feels like trying to stack sand. With every addition it continues to fall down upon itself and cover up what at first was simple inspiration. Make no mistake, art, in any form, may be inspiring and uplifting, enlightening or enraging, but first, it is just plain messy. So controlling the avalanche of the minutia of thoughts that accumulate with the ADD of the creative spirit becomes paramount so as not to impede the function of the space or the freedom to create. You can inadvertently cage your creative spirit with too many extraneous stimuli and render yourself artistically impotent.

Do you remember me giving you the 360-degree tour earlier?

So even now, while I write, I exist in these rooms simultaneously, both physically and intellectually. I sit in these rooms, and between sentences, I look around me at the clutter. The clutter is literally and figuratively the by-product or waste of the leftover bits of things and stuff I once thought I needed but have lost their usefulness or at least their ability to arouse or inspire. My natural belief is that nothing is useless until it no longer exists, so my natural response to the presence of the clutter is to save the remnants and try to breathe life back into them. In actuality, much of the clutter is just that...clutter. The only service clutter provides is to obscure the important things you wish to focus on....hardly a desirable service. So the task now is to sit here in these glorious and frightening wastelands and, step by step, re-imagine the path I intended to follow and find the roadblocks I have placed in my own way. I'm certain some roadblocks will seem huge, so they must be dismantled before they can be removed. Fortunately for me, I own more than one hammer. So it would appear it is also time to view the pilgrimage to the end goals of creation in smaller pieces while maintaining total faith in the grander vision of things.

I must start by reminding myself of the simple purity of inspiration; it comes through me, not from me. I must be ever mindful of the fact that I am not The Creator; I am one who is blessed with the occasional ability to channel the creation. I know, it all sounds like old soul hippie, new age spiritual seeker kind of stuff.....Well, if it walks like a duck, etc., etc.

So, earlier, I asked you to remember those dimensions that constituted a room, height, width and depth. (Here comes more of that hippie stuff) That "room" in your head....has no dimensions to restrict it other than the ones you create for it. That room can be as deep as you like, exploring any emotion you wish. It can be wide enough to encompass all of the life you see and all of the passion you feel. It can be high enough to commune with God himself, if he sees fit, of course. In that room, there is all the space you need for answers, even for the questions that have not yet been asked. A large part of the journey ahead of me is to always be enlarging and remodeling that room but not filling it up with static reminders of perceived limitations. But for now, to get *me rolling in the right direction, I will start by keeping it stupidly simple. I will just get rid of the shoes that are worn out and the pants that don't go around me any longer, books I've already read, and broken things that I will actually never get around to fixing.*

Little victories back-to-back will eventually win this war.

So… as I said before, today I ponder the difference between room and a room, both literally and figuratively. I have both, but at times, both present me with the challenge of making decisions that are confusing at best. These decisions, taken at face value, seem like simple enough choices that could be made with little or no contemplation. That said, every choice has consequences of some description. These could relate to your relationships with people, places, animals, things… the list goes on. The contemplation of consequences is what a logical decision is built on, and you should indeed always consider consequences in your decision-making.

However…..

(look out, fauxlosopher at work)

The continuous contemplation of consequences resulting in an inability to choose is the beginning of the end to progress and, most certainly, the demise of creativity.

So, now I feel like I should be quoting something from Tennyson's The Charge of the Light Brigade… clutter to the left of me, clutter to the right of me, clutter right in front of me… sad that…

Truthfully, you know, cards on the table... I'll tell you now, I started the search for a way to process the mélange of material that has been collected over the years, years ago. I wrote down as many thoughts as I could, but there is still... I was going to say, "a wealth of material" yet to go through. But describing it as wealth might be just a bit misleading unless, of course, you believe, as I do, that one man's trash is another man's treasure.

I have tried to take full advantage of my smartphone and use its voice recorder to make notes for myself. I use it for spoken words as well as musical thoughts. Not every entry will be fleshed out and utilized, but at least it is recorded, and I have not left it up to my memory to be the archivist or gatekeeper. Before I owned a smartphone, I used a micro-cassette recorder and then an MP3 recorder for such things. Now I have hours and hours... and hours... of singular thoughts, rhymes, and melodies to go through. If this book makes me a few bucks, perhaps I will have the time to revisit that stuff. Who knows, my second book could be hiding in there amid the mental overflow.

Sometimes, it is hard to tell if what I have thought will actually be of use to anyone else but me. I do know that I have been touched sometimes by someone else's simple turn of phrase, just a few words strung together that, once heard, settle in my chest, generating a warmth of their own. Hopefully, as this book is being written, I will indeed find my way through the varied clutter, physically, mentally, and spiritually. I wonder if the Marie Kondo method of de-cluttering will work for all three...?

...PUSH DON'T COME TO SHOVE...

Some days are more joyous than others. I mean, I wake up every day with gratitude in my heart just for waking up. It means I have been blessed once again with a chance to better myself and/or someone else right along with me. It also means another day of hearing those tiny voices trying to tell me that things won't change or that I'm somehow not enough of something (depending on the day). I first heard these voices long, long ago when classmates or siblings would make fun of my ears, my scrawny arms, or any of many body parts that, as a pre-pubescent, were lacking in their maturity. But in truth, it could have been anything; kids will tease other kids, and they will make stuff up if there is nothing really that can be singled out. And God forbid you show any emotion over being teased; that just gets you labeled as weak, or a pussy, or a fag.

So, those feelings get repressed; that is the way most of us are wired. But repressed feelings do not mean they have gone away; they are just stacked up, waiting for a time to safely be set free. Sadly, that means that as long as they exist, they have the opportunities to color a great many future actions, reactions, decisions, and relationships. Also, as we grow a little older, we begin to understand larger concepts. For example, financial and/or societal limitations, repressed anger, or fear can color those too. When you begin to understand that those feelings can be dealt with, and do NOT have to color your world anymore, just because that is what they HAVE done up until now... that is when you begin to see with clearer purpose. You must get comfortable with questioning yourself. The questions should take big stuff and little stuff from your past and allow you to look at them from the outside, as a stranger might.

Then, make a determined effort to shed the unimportant, face the deeper feelings, hopefully, thereby finding a way to dissolve its hold on you, making space for new inspirations and blessings. I know... it is easier said than done, but certainly worth the effort.

Push Don't Come to Shove   *(03/2018)*

I'm praying that I'm saying all the right things to convince me that my dreams are waiting for me, to believe that they are true.

Feels like I'm staring at a sign that says, just turn here, and you'll be fine,

But if I follow the road well-traveled, I could wind up waiting in a queue.

What am I doing? Where am I going...what am I missing,

did I pass the exit ramp to fortune somewhere along this road?

In my younger days while still in school, did I miss the class on "follow through,"

Or did I just become distracted in my efforts to fit the mold?

Some days are hard, some harder than others,

and I pray for fewer as I'm growing old.

I wonder, have my apprehensions been caused by slacked attentions?

Could it be I took too long to look outside of what I'd been told?

Coming from a place of toil and grief, where the challenges of living can limit one's belief,

I am learning now that the truth may indeed be the reverse.

So much time spent complaining never noticed it restraining,

so I lived a life of limits well-rehearsed.

I lived a life of certainty that I'd always have just what I need,

now, I see that as a disservice to myself and those I love

When I should have been as certain that there is no wall or curtain,

between me and a life deserving, where push doesn't come to shove

So come one, come all, let blessings fall,

And fill me up with love and thankfulness until the coffers overflow.

Let my soul become imbued with a boundless gratitude

and charge me, share my abundance, with everyone I know.

This is day two spent on this particular piece. Today, I took in a sunrise at the beach with my brother, actually a dear friend that I consider as much of a brother as my biological ones. Anyway, we got our toes in the sand and the water and got a little grounding in. Then, we slipped off to breakfast, where I started telling him about this poem and the inner-child things I was addressing that sort of brought this to the forefront for me.

Well, suddenly, he became very talkative and began to confide in me about his loneliness and self-imposed isolation since his wife's death seven years ago. He said, while I was telling him about all the years I was picked on and beat up, that he had flashbacks to his own childhood. He has dyslexia, and way back then, he was just considered stupid because reading and writing were ferociously hard for him. He was teased and excluded from stuff. But he worked extra hard to keep up and still graduated with his class. He was class President in his junior and senior years. He was a youth group leader for two years at his church, went on to college… But still, somehow, he always felt "less than" his peers. That is imposter syndrome. And that can be based on childhood memories of somehow not being enough. He is still battling with that inner child. As an adult, married, his wife was his proof that he was worthy, that he was indeed enough. But after her death, he slid right back into anonymity.

Okay, so, as we spoke, I asked him if he still prayed, and he said he did. I asked him if he prayed aloud, and he said he didn't. I suggested to him that if, in the privacy of his own home, he could not bring himself to be vocal about his wants or desires, he was fuckin' up. I said, "...you still believe in God the Creator?" He said he did. Then I said, "Well then, for Christ's sake, SPEAK UP, man." I told him that, in my opinion, if he could not "talk" to God and ask for what he wants, then he would likely never find a way out of his isolation. I suggested he be vocal in his conversations with God and the universe at large when he decides to ask for help in letting out the anger and fears from childhood. He said he was a little worried about what the neighbors might think if he got carried away and screamed and cried. I asked if he was planning on being so loud that the neighbors would hear him. He replied, "Not really...but it could happen...".

Sounds to me like he is getting ready to challenge the universe in a cage match to help him out.

Crap, I hope the universe is ready for this...

I feel pretty certain we will be revisiting these topics again: childhood repression, imposter syndrome, and inner voices. What about you? Have you challenged the faith you profess to have, to keep up its end of the bargain in helping you heal, move forward in your dreams, or increase your abundance? Do you have a faith to draw from?

...GREENER PASTURES...

While writing this book, the time frame I find myself in is also the tail end of an election cycle. So naturally, politics are on my mind whether I care for it or not. Much like having a personal relationship with God, which is nobody's business but our own, I see politics in much the same way. I don't feel the need to tell you about mine unless you truly value my opinion and/or experiences...and ask for it. The unsolicited opinion is just being a buttinsky, and nobody likes a buttinsky. Neither am I into debates for the sake of debate. Not to mention that most people don't actually understand the difference between a debate and an argument. Even the televised political debates have little resemblance to what I was taught in school regarding debating decorum.

I do think that I can speak my mind with you about some of my feelings on the subject of politics because a) you bought this book, b) you were warned of my splintered thoughts before you did...and c) besides that, my views politically are much more about the spiritual aspects of "civil service" and the status quo of the degradation therein, rather than a dissertation on the political parties and their respective policies. Yes, I am aware that sounded a little angry. But I swear I'm not mad, disappointed...sure, expectant of better from elected officials...you bet, entertaining mild thoughts and plots of social revenge, could be. And perhaps I am even a little twisted...yes...but not mad. "Bwah-ha-ha-ha," he laughed as he stroked his cat...

Greener Pastures   *(09/2020)*

You begged, come cast your lot with me, have faith I'll speak your will,

But your loyalty is suspect as you step foot upon the hill.

Your promises are now seldom kept once you've settled in your seat

And the open door you promised now collects a toll discrete

Will you be just another who settles for personal gains

Or will you be one of the leaders who finally breaks the chains

Now I'm growing to be mistrusting of the bulk of what you say

As I see rights eroding and more in peril every day

Tax breaks for the wealthiest, with promises of what "could be."

If we let them use that money to bolster our economy

But that promise never does pan out, never sees the light of day

They gift the dollars to themselves, and all calmly look away

The greenery of pastures new, make drowned this voice of mine,

Until you become a stranger to my heart and to my mind.

Do you think that we don't notice how your pockets start to bulge

When you turn your back on those who lack, as the wealthy you indulge

When you control our country's wealth and have the power to decide its use

Will you wager the security of future generations by playing it fast and loose

Once was the people had a voice that had a chance to shine

Until the thieves grew louder, with gifts and cash and wine

We are still here, the working poor who struggle every day

But losing as the power of wealth makes you look the other way

Will you still hear the voices of those you promised to protect

Or give more credit to the gamblers and leave us to pay their debts

Day 4 of this thought…

I was quite distracted from my own path for the last two days by the onslaught of social media concerning politics. I am amazed and disappointed by how many people I know suddenly feel free to post (mostly re-post) the most outrageous memes you can imagine. I am certain that the people who are creating these things have only two goals in mind: one is to garnish cheap laughter from insulting text or images, and the second is to create further division between people. It's surprising how easy that is to do when disguised as humor. I took some time trying to find an analogy for the way these troubling memes are used… bear with me…

I am making a broad assumption here in that I think almost everyone, at some point in their childhood, was bullied by one or more kids (as in Push Don't Come to Shove). And you remember when I said that if you showed emotion concerning the bullying, i.e., anger or tears… or both… then the bullies won because they had made you feel smaller still. Ladies and Gentlemen, I put forth to you that all of this left-handed political crap we are bombarded with on social media is exactly the same kind of psychological mind-fuck that bullies used on us before. It caused a lot of kids to become wallflowers, retreating in silence and choosing to not participate in a world that should have been theirs to enjoy as well. I know where social media is concerned, I often find myself choosing silence over confrontation with a faceless irritant.

What I find MORE confusing is how many of these people who post and re-post this poison profess to be "Christian" and still take part in this mass marketing of hatred. (I know…they're only jokes, right?…that's what the schoolyard bullies used to say, too, "we're just kidding around"…) We all hated bullies in school…so why do we tolerate them now?

I guess what I'm really trying to say is… if any of you who were bullied in school for any reason, and remember what that felt like, and are now the ones currently designing, posting or re-posting these hateful examples of humanity, who's only purpose is to create anger and division; congratulations you are now one of the bullies…

you just wait until your heavenly Father gets home…

...ENLIGHTENMENT AND BS...

Today, there are many things going on in my life—some good, some great, some annoying—but all in the name of growth. I feel that a great many more things are happening behind the scenes for my betterment, things I may not even be aware of. It has often been the case for me, perhaps for most of us, perhaps for all of us. It rather depends on the individual and whether he or she expects that kind of "divine" assistance. I suppose that is a definition of sorts for faith. I continue to plant the seeds for a more abundant future and try not to keep rethinking them once I've done so. This is not always easy.

I woke up feeling like today is the day I give you the outline of events that have shaped my reality for the last few years. But I wondered... if I do that, am I, in essence, reminding myself of pain or disappointments that I have said I already dealt with and let go? I'll assume this push-you-pull-me thought process is ongoing for most of us and, frankly, delves into deeper psychology... which I am not qualified to write about. I can only tell you about me here and now, and I hope perhaps there is something tucked away inside the words I write that resonates with something inside of you and helps you to see your own truth somewhere between the lines. I suppose therein lies a question for anyone trying to get beyond their past and live in the present in gratitude.

Are you living in faith that where you are now is exactly where you need to be to move forward in your journey to a more complete and fulfilling life?

Trust me, I know that this is beginning to sound like a hundred other things you've read about being thankful for living in the present and "making peace" with your past. But since so many videos and publications cover these same philosophies, it is tricky not to sound like the last thing that might have inspired you. Often, I write a little something on the topics of faith, gratitude, enlightenment, soul-searching, or any other topic that is somehow instantly assumed to be "old hippie" stuff. Should I decide to post it online, it is always met with an odd array of comments. It may get a couple of likes, or a share, or a few comments—usually of agreement or support. But sometimes, I am met with a reader who sees me as a threat to themselves because they somehow see my opinions as a threat to the "American way of life," their life, or a threat to "Christian values"—their values. In my defense, I do not see anything I write as dangerous to America, or Christianity for that matter. Furthermore, if you see my mental ramblings as a threat, then in my opinion, either your faith or the institutions themselves are already in danger of collapsing like a house of cards, and you are afraid I might just say something that peeks through your windows or shakes the table.

Enlightenment and BS   *(08/2018)*

Let me start by saying…… In my opinion, enlightenment is NOT Bullshit! As a matter of fact, in my opinion, by broad definition, enlightenment is the polar opposite. It is also NOT dumb shit, horse shit, stupid shit, useless shit or New Age shit. Enlightenment is the journey through all that and more since man understood he had a consciousness and formulated the notion of sentience. It just did not always have this name. And once it was named, it has indeed adopted different meanings throughout the ages.

During the 17th and 18th centuries, the Western concept of enlightenment was an intellectual movement based on reason and science as the means by which to understand the world around us. That enlightenment was meant to displace much of the mystical world's explanations for life's questions. So, it did little to address the metaphysical world or the inner workings of the mind, as Eastern religions had done for centuries prior.

It seems to me that now, the term enlightenment is the culmination of all previous definitions. Much like in the world of gastronomy (…that's foodie speak for, well, the science of cooking

81

food), fusion cuisine is the combination of two separate ethnic dishes, which are combined to create an innovative take on both, i.e., Tex-Mex or Euro-Asian. In much the same way that people have different likes or dislikes when it comes to what they eat, some people, the adventurous eaters, will embrace the changes and challenges of the new flavors, while traditionalists will not.

So I guess you could say that "my" take on enlightenment sort of says, Yes, I accept science - yes, I accept logic and reason - yes, I accept that there is far more going on around me than I am able to see - and yes, I believe I can be taught/trained/allowed to see beyond the accepted physical limitations of this world into which I was born. As well as all of the above, my personal enlightenment (...rather like a personal relationship with God) also includes my understanding that in some way, shape or form, intentionally or unintentionally, we are actually players in the struggle for truth and understanding, while dealing with "worldly bullshit". And the end goal of enlightenment, which only likely really happens in the next plane of existence or further still, is to divest yourself of the layers of shit in your life so that your spirit can breathe freely and perhaps help guide you through the physical and emotional restrictions of the world, and enhance your life in some fashion.

Now, my personal fauxlosophy... You may have become a part of the worldly bullshit unintentionally through the act of existence in a particular geography. Or you may have become trapped in a life of debt and /or subservient behavior because your responsibilities require that you play by the ever-changing rules of materialism. Or you may be forced to live by the rules of a society you did not build. In all of these cases, then the shit is merely "on" you. If this is the case, then you can begin a journey to enlightenment in numerous ways. You can start by simplifying your life, minimizing your waste, and being aware of the potential damages of misplaced words and hastened actions. You can begin with prayer, no matter what your mother church may be. You can learn to meditate and always strive to honor humanity in general in your decision-making.

Some portions of enlightenment are truly irritating, for example, growing to understand that every purchase you make for your well-being or comfort in some fashion supports a person, persons or a corporation. And it is possible that they, the people profiting from your purchases, may be conducting their business in a way that is the antithesis of your journey to peace and understanding. Even harder to swallow is the fact that most of us around the world have governments that will cheat, steal, kill and even take part in toppling other governments for long-term material gains. And if you live in such a country, its government monikers notwithstanding, and pay taxes which in turn support its military, which is likely the arm of the government perpetrating such things...then in some fashion, you must own a share of the blame for all of the things that government does.

That is one piece of knowledge that my search for enlightenment left with me that I still struggle with but must accept. All of the aforementioned falderal are pertinent to those who are more victims than victors in their personal lives.

But, and it is very large but, on the other side of that coin, if you have knowingly, willingly become a part of the shit by intentionally helping to create the traps that others must live in or live with, then the shit is "in" you. If you have stolen or cheated someone out of even a little of their livelihood, then the shit is "in" you. If you have ever taken a life or beaten someone horribly for any other reason than self-defense, the shit is "in" you. I fear that should you now decide to recreate your life (and you probably should), your journey will require more of you. Your journey may well be shrouded by shadows of your deeds or the smog you helped to create, and it is possible that much harder lessons await you along the way to your own enlightenment........but the journey is still desirable, the journey is still very real and in the end the journey is still attainable. So no, although some would have you believe otherwise, enlightenment isn't bullshit; it's "The Shit."

If you are at all interested in the political realm, then you know certain words in our language have been re-appropriated for use as weapons in an ideological war. People have affixed brand-new definitions to words to "tag" a particular person or idea as evil, ignorant, or subversive. I mean, I have been called a socialist because I believe in the need for a national healthcare system. I have been called a communist because I believe in some form of wealth distribution. Nothing radical, mind you—just that ALL Americans AND corporations should be paying their taxes just like the working class does. Hell, I even believe that churches should pay taxes if they want a voice in government (which they should not). I also believe that the interest on long-term "credit" purchases needs to be capped and heavily regulated. I have been called a Libtard because I believe in a woman's right to her own body, and because saying the word liberal while sneering is not insulting enough. They had to mash it up with a more offensive word to make clear they equate my socio-political views with those of a mentally challenged person.

All I want to do is suggest that if you have found yourself using any word as a weapon politically, socially, or spiritually—a word intended to denigrate someone else or their point of view—take the time to grab a dictionary and look up the actual meaning of certain words. You will see that they have been grossly perverted to sometimes elicit violent emotion in place of a discussion on social or ideological differences. Those perverted words are meant to be walls, stopping the possibility of compromise. So there, whether you want to be or not, now you too are enlightened. Okay, maybe a little...

...INTERMISSION...

SURPRISE!!

I know, right...?...providing an intermission in the middle of a book is not normal. Well, very few people have ever accused me of being normal...so there you go.

Also, there is an outside chance that you are one of those people who gets to reading a good book (and I'm going to assume of course, that this is one of them) and loses track of time. If that is you...then... HEY! Take a break! You have been reading for a while now and could really use a stretch or maybe a bathroom trip. Go get a beer, or a coffee, or cheesecake (I don't know you...) before reading any further...or don't...I really don't care. But at least now I've done my part...

At any rate....consider the following offerings much the same as you would the dancing hotdog and popcorn onscreen at the theater, cute but wholly unnecessary...

...origami dragons...

I received a package one day via messenger, with no clue as to where it had come from. Little by little I opened it (...could have been a bomb, I don't know...) and inside was a book and a letter. The letter instructed me to read the book because in it answers to all manner of mysteries, large and small, would be revealed...cool.

...so I began reading... The book smacked of Eastern philosophy mixed with just a touch of what I perceived to be perhaps Druid or Wicca by nature. A few dozen pages into the text, it was rambling on about the spiritual centers of the universe and how we are always "just passing through" until we become enlightened enough to choose where we want to be.

When I got to page 42, I discovered a cutout in the pages, creating a hidden compartment within the book. In the compartment was a piece of paper folded origami-style into a delicate-looking dragon. In ridiculously small print down the dragon's spine, it read, "Open me with all due caution."

I very carefully unfolded the dragon (which took some time, I don't mind telling you) and written inside was, "See page 375 for YOUR answer". C'mon ...how could this be? How could someone I've never met, who published this book in (wait a minute...) in 1962, have any clue as to an answer that I needed when I myself was still essentially ignorant of the question? That being said, I quickly grew as excited to discover this "answer" as I was confused about the possibility of its simple existence. I was truly hoping to be gobsmacked by some mind-blowing revelation. So I anxiously flipped through the pages only to find that the book ended at page 374.

...fuck...

Understandably frustrated, I cursed the book and my gullibility. If I knew where this had come from I would have returned it by throwing it through their window. I crumpled the once beautiful little Dragon with manic body English liken to an epileptic episode. I threw it upon the ground, stomped it flat, and stuffed it back into the void in the book. I slammed the book shut, thinking later I would probably burn the damn thing, just as a matter of principle.

I then, almost instantly, felt foolish for destroying the little dragon. I mean, I could have carefully folded it back up and placed it back in the book, then sent it off to a friend that I would find pleasure in pissing off. Oh well, hindsight...

So what is the moral of this little story, you may ask...??... I don't know... never trust an origami dragon?

...the roots of doubt...

I have been in heavy reflection for the last several weeks trying to determine what is holding me back from going after the artist's life I'm certain I am supposed to be living. I am finding a lot of simple doubts have their roots in my childhood, even though my childhood was amazing. I apparently have some issues to overcome, nothing violent or overtly traumatic in any way, but nonetheless shaping the person I would one day become.

Some of these things probably did a number on my self-esteem in some fashion and helped to create the imposter syndrome that I deal with from time to time.

For example, I spent most of my adolescence in snow country with a definite handicap. While not obvious to just anyone who looked at me, there was this thing that separated me from many of my peers, and for me, it was a real challenge to overcome.

You see, I could not then, nor can I now, pee in a straight line. Go ahead and laugh; it's funny to me now, too, but back then...back then, it was hysterical to my friends which made me feel quite self-conscious. You see when I pee, it comes out spinning and sort of fans out a bit. I know that doesn't sound like a real handicap; bear with me. So in the winter, when all the other boys were droppin' trow, grabbin' their peckers, and writing their names in the snow...   I had to first learn calligraphy.

...some thoughts on thoughts...

and the creators of internal dialogue

I find moments like this fascinating... by that, I mean moments when I sit to write, and the thoughts presented by my internal dialogue are flowing freely as though they were already written down somewhere and my fingers were reading them as they typed them.

By vocation, I am a blue-collar artist (specializing in artistic construction); my days are filled with problem-solving. I am charged with the responsibility of taking someone else's vision and figuring out how to bring it into being in the physical world. This task requires my internal dialogue to be a roundtable discussion, dissecting the cause and effect of multiple solutions to any given puzzle. I am required to think outside the box or even ignore the box completely.

Then, I have to wrangle all of those thoughts, sift through them, choose a course of action, and try to get them all moving in the same direction.

For years, my avocation has been that of a singer/ songwriter/poet/visual artist. My internal dialogue therein is the driver of the creation of art in multiple forms. Before cellphones, I began carrying a personal recording device because when an idea came up "in my head" and it logically felt like it may have had merit, I would record the thought because there was no guarantee that I would think of it again. At some later time, I could review these thoughts when there was time for the internal roundtable discussion. Consequently, I still have dozens and dozens of hours of recorded ideas that I visit every other month or so and attempt to weed them out a little more.

I used to think that I may be a little tetched because of the constant dialogue in my head, especially the occasional dark thoughts. Then, I came to an understanding, if you will, about thoughts in general, and it has shaped my thoughts on thoughts ever since. That understanding is as follows: we have "little to no control" over our thoughts, that is to say, our initial thoughts. Initial thoughts brought forth in our minds are coming through us, not from us. An initial thought can be so far removed from every outside influence that it may seem completely alien to us. The control we have over thought only comes after the initial thought, and our decisions to follow that thought through or dismiss it as meaningless or unwanted. If we did indeed have control over our thoughts, I could tell you exactly what I would be thinking 30 minutes from now... but I can't even tell you what my next thought will be.

(...so there I was, in the elevator, having sex with a smoking hot amputee when.... NOPE...not following that one... but sadly, there is now a permanent placeholder in my brain for it... and even stranger than that, there is more than likely one in your brain now also... I'm sorry, or.... you're welcome...)

We can train our brains not to respond negatively to a negative thought, but we are, from time to time, going to experience negative thoughts. The basic truth about this matter concerning thoughts is that we are all creators in both a spiritual and material sense. We live inside a mental world we create for ourselves based on our experiences. I create endlessly, and so do you. Now, I know I have said this in conversations before, but it is important that it be said often when it comes to our experiences and creations.

The vast majority of everything you have ever had, owned, experienced, or consumed (yes... even a great deal of what you now eat) had its beginning as a thought somewhere in someone else's mind. A chain of events, fostered by additional thoughts that followed that original thought, brought it into reality. It may have taken years or even generations to happen... but it did. Other than in nature itself, ALL THINGS began somewhere, at some time, because somebody had a thought.

Anyway.... Now that I have rattled on about my particular fauxlosophy let me finish with this: as an artist, I was once questioned about where inspiration comes from, and my reply was, "...you never know where inspiration will find you. You must allow your thoughts the freedom to wander and document their travels."

A great thought, especially for those who are procrastinators by nature. But, we all should find some way to document our thoughts other than strictly on social media platforms. Document them in a way that will allow you to revisit them at your leisure and investigate them more thoroughly. Not all creations are meant for anyone else to see. Some creations are silly or borderline absurd, and some creations can be downright profound. Some creations are meant to free ourselves from something holding us in a place of zero growth and some creations are meant to do that for somebody else, someone we may never meet, another great reason to always be creating.

I love you all, and if you are creating (and we all do with our every thought) then document the travels and share the positive ones with the world. As often as possible, be aware of the world you are creating with your thoughts. Practice being aware of the thoughts you give your energies to. Try to remain conscience of creating out of a place of love.

You never know when one of your thoughts, one of your creations, could even briefly and without your knowledge become someone else's reality. Let's work to make those potential realities ones of boundless love and cooperation. Let's create a world brave enough to be unafraid of our own vulnerabilities. If we can do that, then we can be compassionate to one another and help one another to grow stronger still.   ...Now, back to our show...

...MORNINGS WITH MY SISTER...

Lately, I have been very distracted by thoughts of a woman. We actually barely know one another, and perhaps I should not be having such intense daydreams about her... but I am, so... there you go. The more I thought about whether or not it was decent of me to entertain such indecent thoughts about her, the more I became convinced that it is likely NOT unusual at all. But I can only speak from a guy's perspective where this is concerned. I mean, I am still assuming that "I" am much like most guys in the way I think about sex... which is a great deal... and a fair amount of the time in any given day. If you give me thirty minutes of mostly idle time, it is almost a certainty that some sort of sexual thought will occur within those thirty minutes. And while I have felt compelled to write these thoughts down, I will have to share them in another book dedicated to literature of the "blue" variety.

I will share this with you, though: a little something I jotted down about a phone conversation I had with my sister one morning.

Mornings with my Sister   *(05/2020)*

Although I have still been posting random thoughts on social media, my "real" writing has been in a bit of a slump. So I was online searching for a full moon incantation to try and coax my muse back to me. I was beginning to feel like I needed to apologize to her for wasting my time on other interests. That is when my sister messaged me....

Her: Morning Sunshine!! Are you up and cranking out the creative juices??

Me; ...well, this morning has been unfocused. It has encompassed a little research on Reishi mushrooms (which are sprouting wild in the area right now) ...sociopolitical dissertation and banter on a newly liked FB page, videos from Chef and Farmer about grits and rice... and...soft porn. I think my muse is on strike. I figure the creative juices will start flowing just about the time I am supposed to be starting the weekend's yard work...I guess we'll see how that goes...

Her; LOL... stick with the porn. It's way more fun than yard work! (at least short-term) Have a great day, my precious...Love You Madly!!

Me; ...in as much as I want to be inspiring in a political or social fashion, it seems my muse is just an unrepentant, bodacious southern broad, hard-to-embarrass, and she recognizes little to no difference between the pleasures derived from sex or biscuits and gravy, or smooth liquor...I am missing her badly.

Her: Oh, a "simple girl,"...how refreshing. I will leave you to your pleasures, nudge, nudge, wink, wink... I totally get how important focus is at your age (smiley face)

Me...sadly true, it requires more focus than it used to just to pee...

Her: LOL...well, get back to work "at hand."

...I love our little talks...

Yes, I do have conversations about sex and intimacy with my sisters and with my daughter, too, for that matter. It is how I keep abreast (no pun intended) of how women really feel about certain things where men are concerned. Come to think of it, there is a distinct possibility that these women are not exactly a "proper sampling" of women in general. I mean, they will talk to me about anything: morning boners, probiotics, lady-wood, UTIs, how much time passes before foreplay gets boring, pick-your-own fruit farms near them, which Denny's in their town is best, orgasms and more stuff like that.

As a matter of fact, my older sister told me something when I was in my twenties that has served me quite well since. She said,

"...there are almost as many varieties of sex as there are people who are having sex. If you are in a relationship with somebody that you truly trust, then you should never be embarrassed or afraid to ask for what you want to experience. No matter how far out the initial thought is, it is really only "kinky" the first time. Then you decide to either abandon that thought for the future...or do it again because you both got a charge out of it.

Best sex advice ever!!

...MORNING COMES...

Oh, what the hell. Since we have sort of broached the subjects of love and lust, here is a little something with shades of blue for you. It is actually a love poem, a rather steamy love poem. But don't worry; it is only pornographic if your mind has no difficulty comprehending sexual innuendo or reading between the lines for "intention." And if, by chance, this gets your motor going, and you think you may have an appetite for more, then get on my mailing list, and I'll let you know if and when the blue book is coming out. Just enter "take me now" in the subject line, and I'll keep you on my naughty list.

So, when I write about matters of intimacy, I usually feel I need to be guarded to some extent. Even when I wrote sexy notes and letters to my wife, I did not want to sound harsh and unfeeling, like a low-budget porn film. Even after years of marriage, I was still timid when it came to talking dirty. I can write it like a son-of-a-bitch, but saying stuff while having sex never came easy to me. I wanted to be like a very hot love letter, but the fear that it would just come out more like graffiti held me back. I want to paint a beautiful picture, every brushstroke creating a visage of a lovely, lustful, albeit messy scene, and when the moment is upon me, all I've got is spray paint...

And while I can talk to my sister and my daughter about sex and stuff, there is no way I'm going to ask them what kind of dirty talk works for them. While I'm certain it would be enlightening in some respect, chances are that if I used that information in the act, I might think of them, and that would not be okay. So, maybe the next woman in my life will help me out with this conundrum.

Morning Comes *(05/2021)*

Awaken me with a gentle touch
That leaves no question in its stead
That you desire me as much
And coax the slumber from my head

Awaken you, exploring hands.
Claiming your ascendancy
Enrapture me with your demands
Solicit shameless revelry

Awaken me and take me in
Your fearful passion circumvent
Let not your inhibition win
Play me, your willing instrument

Awaken you; my lust entreat
There is no place from which to fall
Let timid doubt lie at your feet
And know that I have dreamed it all

Awaken me if so inclined.
Make me the object of your urge
Loose every wicked, playful thought
Allow your fantasies to purge
Awaken you plead me devour

Cause me to rise with a whispered voice

To glom a slice of these wee hours

And know 'tis you that owns the choice

Awaken me with wanton lips.

With a knowing grin and impish eyes

With tender hands and fingertips

As the morning comes before sunrise

See what I mean: I can write stuff that is kind of sexy.

Hmmm, now I'm thinking about dedicating a web page to this book for open discussions from readers. Maybe I could take advice from strangers where my shortcomings are concerned; maybe others could as well. I mean, hopefully, if such a space existed, more than just sex would get discussed. After all, this book is about much more than just that. Who knows, by the time this book is published, all of these ideas will be more than wishful thinking, more than "what if." Keep checking in with Marginal Prophet Publishing on your favorite social media; you never know.

...EMPATHETIC
OBSERVERS...

You know, when I started writing this book, it was my intention to tell my readers what inspires me. I intended to offer my thoughts in sort of a "real-time" format. Whatever a day brought to me that prompted new writings or reminded me of things I had already written, that is what I wanted to explore. And then, somewhere along the line, it began to feel like I was acting like a life coach or something. So, I decided I would take a step back, look at what progress I had made in writing this book, and do a little self-examination to determine if I had indeed strayed from the original intent for this book.

So, I spent the better part of two days really trying to be objective about my work. I asked myself questions like, "Have I learned enough to claim valuable insight into the human condition?"... no, not really. I have only opinions.

Does that mean that "my" thoughts on the subject do not have merit where these things are concerned? Not really. I'm entitled to my own opinions.

Do those opinions have enough validity on their own to be considered worthwhile? ... I don't know, I can't know. At least, I can't know unless I share them with others and see if "they" can validate them.

Wait... have others "validated" them? ... am I truly reliant on the opinion of others where my opinions are concerned? That question turned over and over in my mind for hours. It turns out that intellectually, the answer to that question is a resounding... no. I mean, I'm not an idiot; certainly, my opinions have been formed through a logical balancing of pros and cons over years of contemplation. But emotionally?... ... emotionally, the answer could sound more like... maybe.

So why, then, do I question myself? Why do I still deal with "imposter's syndrome" from time to time? Why do I sometimes feel as though I may need to offer somebody, somewhere, an apology for wasting their time with my creative rants? All reasonable questions to entertain, but infuriating to do so. Nobody on the face of the planet, unless they are a narcissistic sociopath, has ever NOT had self-doubt. So why does this type of doubt feel so personally harmful? Is there any upside to experiencing self-doubt?

I am not (intentionally) a life coach, a teacher, a therapist or a spiritual advisor. But I have been, individually, all of these things to someone at some point in time. Unless you are a hermit or live in a state of self-imposed social isolationism, then you have been one or more of these things to someone at some point in time as well. Has anyone ever asked for your opinion or your advice?... Booyah!...see? You're a teacher, too.

So now that you know that about yourself, let's double back to whether there is any upside to experiencing self-doubt.

So, my opinion, my answer to that question is Yes...it appears there is an upside; it just doesn't reveal itself in a grandiose fashion. There is no "voila," no epiphany, no "Aha" moment. But if you accept the fact that you will have self-doubt from time to time and try to look at the reason for experiencing it, then it may indeed be helpful. It may point to a place where you know on a subconscious level that you could have done much better. And if that causes you to try harder and causes you to be more mindful in your words or actions, then yes, it has an upside. Self-doubt can be a great motivator. It can be useful in your relationships with family and friends if it opens your mind to be more accepting of their feelings or their opinions. It can be useful on the job if you use it as a tool for establishing the quality of your work. Self-doubt is only an issue that needs professional help if it is debilitating, daily preventing you from even trying to achieve.

So, a few paragraphs back, I said I was trying hard to be objective about my work. Well, it turns out that where creatives are concerned, self-doubt is just part of the program. And because we are very often looking inward to capture the spark for creating, the vast majority of us cannot be objective about our work.

Our views of our artistic offerings are always going to be subjective, and that is just fine. Often, we are our own worst critics. Sadly, for people who deal with self-esteem issues, they may be harder on themselves than is probably needed. If we cannot be completely objective about our own work, it's okay as long as we allow the rest of the world their objectivity where our work is concerned.

Empathetic Observers   *(09/2020)*

Drawing pictures with letters until words drip with colors,
Crafting music from silence that waits to be heard.
A comfort to some but disturbing to others
My soul on display to the world

Anxious to learn, always listening, praying.
Trying to glean truth from my left and my right
The weight of the task as empathic observer
Means you feel all the pain, but you don't get to fight

As an artist, my charge, is to somehow see beyond me
To not forget the power of images and words
To step outside the mirrored halls that would see me as the center
To use these gifts in light and love to ease a worried world

To challenge just one mind to be more introspective
Perhaps they'll see the fences they have built around their hearts

I hope to offer visions from multiple perspectives

If I can vanquish just one fear, then I'll have done my part

If you ask for my opinions, I will share them

But opinions are just that, and neither swine nor pearls

I'd rather share my dreams and hope that others dream as I do

Impossible as it seems, my dream is peace around the world

So, you say that it's impossible, and you won't waste your time

It's senseless to try to imagine our weary world at peace

Well, I say if you can't bring yourself to even try imagining

You may well be part of the reason that it stays out of reach

So, where does that leave me today? It leaves me remembering two people from my formative years, for whom I will forever be grateful. I had two teachers in high school who made great impressions on me where art is concerned. I had an English teacher/drama coach named Carmen Adkins, who never let her actors get away with delivering a line without properly emoting emotion. She would say, "You must project not only your voice to the back of the theater, but I want to hear the projection of emotion from back here as well." So, now, when creating music, I often remember that instruction. I try to convey the emotion that may have spawned the work in every performance of that work.

Then, there was my art teacher, James Rush, who helped me understand where art resides within us and what it means to let it flow through us. He was also the guy who taught me how to let others have their own opinions about my work. He said, art and inspiration come through you, not from you. You get to be the vessel that turns a thought or vision into something tactile. But as an artist, you must remember that once you feel you are done with a piece and make it available for others to see (and hopefully own), its ownership is no longer yours. It is now something others are invited to view, ponder, and feel in any way that they want to about it. Some will love it, some may hate it, and the rest will just be indifferent to it, not caring to take the time to look long enough to feel it. All of them are completely acceptable responses.

So, if you are or intend to be a creator of some form, take those little gems with you, enjoy the opportunities, and be grateful for the gifts you get to share.

It took me far too long to understand and accept that my particular gifts could indeed have some value to someone, somewhere, beyond mere financial recompense. It goes beyond the ideas and ideals that mortal man has put into operation in the physical world. Sometimes, you do get direct feedback from someone concerning the effect that your words or work had on them. But there are going to be many more instances when what you have put out into the world has affected someone else's life, perhaps dramatically, and you may never know about it.

So, be mindful of what you put out in the world.

...ALL THE TIME IN THE WORLD...

I started my day listening to classic rock music from the early 1960s through the late 70s. I had almost forgotten about some of these brilliantly written songs. I am talking about the ones with social messages or actual stories to tell. I find myself wondering about the skills of those songwriters who seemed able to write a protest song without being completely literal in their verbiage, with descriptions of their political bias or specifics of war or hunger. Of course, not all of them could do it or could do it all of the time, but still, it takes a real poet to pull that off.

Now, because you have read this far in this book, you know I do indeed delve into the world of politics, but rarely, if ever, will I speak of policies or specific politicians. Instead, I will usually try to share my thoughts on what is missing from the "body" of government or politics. And in most cases, that is a heart, and a soul.

Hmm... the "body" of government or politics... I believe there may be something to explore here. Our government continues to allow more of the "personal rights guaranteed by the Bill of Rights to individuals" to be given to corporations in this country, thus allowing those with ample wallets to spend vast amounts of money aimed at getting their favorite candidates into office. And that big money being allowed into the election system continues to reduce the "individual" rights by controlling the "choices" available to us. You can mull that one over, and perhaps we will look at that closer...later... for now, I digress...

What follows is today's inspiration set to verse and is becoming a song right along with the drafting of this book.

All the Time in the World   *(08/11/24)*

Wondering how we got this far this fast,

without noticing the things that were going south

Wondering how much longer we can last,

Without shoring up the damage to this house

   We keep acting like we've got all the time in the world,

   to make things right

   But we put off making changes, citing comfort

   and all we seem to do is fight

You know I really want to see it,

all the things we profess to be, be true, for everyone

You know, I feel like I'm pissing in the wind when I ask if we can start again

And all you ever say is it can't be done

   We keep acting like we've got all the time in the world,

   to make things right

   And if we could agree to think with more than just our wallets

   There exists a chance we might

      If we put off tough decisions,

      and don't try to make the changes where it counts

      Then power mongers just grow stronger,

      And that makes them so much harder to denounce

   I think I know what you think of me, and you think I'm naïve and cannot see

How hard it is, to get things done

But if you choose to not even try, then you're a big part of the reasons why,

This battle for civility can't be won

    We keep acting like we've got all the time in the world,

    to make things right

    With my ignorance a given, there still exists the chance,

    That you too, might be short on sight

        I'm not looking left or right

        And I'm not trying to start a fight; I'm just afraid

        If we can't find a middle ground

        Then this country that we love might just wind up DOA

We keep acting like we've got all the time in the world

We keep acting like we've got all the time in the world

We keep acting like we've got all the time in the world

Can we stop acting like we've got all the time in the world

Can we stop acting like we've got all the time in the world

Can we just stop

Well, I have read over what I wrote today, both the lyrics and what I wrote about the lyrics. And I must say, now it feels like I've challenged myself to be more outspoken. I did not wake up today feeling like I needed a new challenge, and to be honest, I'm not certain I like the feeling. I mean politicians have their own staff writers to meticulously pour over every line, every word to be certain they are not contradicting themselves along the way, not saying too much in detail, not saying too little. As an artist or creator of any description, there is rarely a team to guide us. We have not hired a publicist to run interference or an advance team to remove tripping hazards as we move forward. Nor is there usually a rear guard to watch our backs.

So, I will take some time to ponder this. If you too, get the feeling that you should be more outspoken about your feelings somewhere, not necessarily politics, take your time to make yourself clear, perhaps clearer than I have made myself. And unless it is your goal to do so, take the time to be certain that you are not speaking in such a fashion as to prompt an immediate defensive response from anyone. It is not cowardice to purposefully avoid that type of tit-for-tat. It is essential to recognize it and understand that that is where communication stops, and arguments begin. And let's be honest about it... we never actually get anywhere meaningful through arguing.

it would appear that I cannot not sound like a life coach. You would think that I would learn...but like I said before, there are times I could really use a handler...

...PIECES OF PUZZLES...

I laid in bed this morning, drifting in and out of awareness, somewhere between awake and asleep, wishing sleep would win out. I reached over to where my wife used to sleep beside me, patted the mattress, and found memories of her there. For the briefest of moments, I felt she was near enough to hear me, and I her, if she decided to speak to me. Then, as the gentle early morning anxiety concerning things undone tried to take hold, I just spoke to her instead. I reminded her that I loved her still and missed her, and then I began apologizing... She has been gone for three years now, and I am afraid that I have let the home she created for us lose its shine. As a single, aging, distracted man, my housekeeping skills are not nearly what she or this house was used to.

I have messes all about me, where I began the work of clearing out what no longer served me and new intentions for my life. As I lay there in bed with well-worn, spinning thoughts, I began to understand once again that the vast majority of the clutter in my house was just that: clutter. I have an enormous supply of relatively unimportant objects that, at one time, had a purpose, even if it was minimal. But so much of this stuff has not been touched since before her passing. What was it that kept me working in circles around this stuff, often just moving them from one place to another in the guise of progress?

I have shelves of books I have not and will not read. Now, they only serve to remind me that I have made weak promises to myself that I have failed to keep. A great many things around me suggest a similar failing. Until today, when I looked at things I no longer needed or had not used, I saw myself gathering them together and trying to sell them.

But this morning, I've begun to see them in a different light. This morning I've begun to see them as perhaps missing pieces in someone else's life. For instance, I have three very nice suits, of which I have only worn one once. There may be a guy out there who is trying to rebuild his life and needs a suit or two for his new

106

job. I have many toys and games around my house that my grandchildren have long outgrown. I could be donating them to a local shelter for families, and their kids could still find some joy in them. I have tools that I am too old to use; at a garage sale, I might get fifty bucks for the lot of them, but to some young guy trying to get a business off the ground, a gift of them would feel like a miracle.

So, when I did finally climb out of bed, I got myself some coffee and decided to write about this morning's mini cyclone of grief, self-pity, assumed self-importance…well, you get the gist. That is what prompted what you just read. And as I wrote it became a vivid realization that many things I have and do not use are just what somebody else truly needs in their life. As far as the feeling that I was letting my late wife down, where her hard work and homemaking were concerned...it was replaced by my imagining her smile as I tried to help others by gifting these things.

When I thought more about "pieces" of people's lives, I was reminded of a little something I wrote about that very topic.

I'm hoping she will still stand beside me while I continue to get busy with a new life. After all, that is what my wife directed me to do before her passing.

Pieces of Puzzles   *(05/2024)*

I am…

We are all puzzles in various stages of completion. From the beginning, we attempt to find the corners and borders and work our way around and around, getting closer to the center as we live and learn.

Sometimes, other people fall into our lives, and they help find and fill in the missing pieces. Sometimes, we discover that their puzzle and our own become one picture. I did indeed have someone in my life who helped me with mine as I helped her with hers, and we learned as years passed that we did indeed have a very large puzzle together.

It took a long time to build this very involved puzzle, but we were almost there. There were only a few pieces left on the table when suddenly, something jarred the table terribly. The puzzle cracked, and the last of the pieces were dashed to the floor. Luckily, I am not a quitter. Luckily, I remember how beautiful the puzzle was looking.

I am fairly confident that I can push and mush all the pieces on the table together again. Luckily, I have enough light around me to find the missing pieces and maybe complete the puzzle. When this puzzle is finally finished, it is likely to be a little dirty, a little worn, and maybe a few tear stains around the edges, but it is still our puzzle…

I loved it when it was new and I loved it still when it was not, and I will continue to love it even if there is that one missing piece. Because you see, I will always remember what that piece looked like and how it fit into my puzzle. Strange though, that missing piece sometimes seems to be a piece of me she kept for herself, and sometimes it feels like a piece of her that I will always carry around with me. I would bet you money that if she and I could compare the pieces we carry around, they would probably look exactly the same. Except perhaps hers may have a little extra glow to it these days.

She used to love puzzles…

I don't believe there is much more to say about this, except… Anyone who comes into my life now will just have to understand that my love for my late wife will never be diminished. Should there ever be a new love in my life, I would like to think it will be as wonderful and exciting in its own way. And hopefully she will be the type of person that understands puzzles are meant to be fun...

...DAYS GO BY...

The previous offering dealt with time, love, and loss. But it also spoke of faith in some respect. Because I look at most things in my life, at least in part, through spiritual spectacles, it makes sense that I would do the same in discussions of time, love, loss, and even procrastination. I'm sure you will see more of these topics as we go forward. But for now, here are the lyrics to a song I wrote in May of 2021, just a few short months before my wife's death.

It used to feel strange to write something only to rediscover it later and have it mean more to me. Well, it no longer feels strange because I have learned to give up the spiritual ownership of my works, even though this song was as much about my spiritual salvation as it was about my wife's influence on my life.

I'm certain that for somebody, somewhere, these things will mean something special to them. I find a great deal of joy in that.

Days Go By   *(05/2021)*

Days blow by like the wind sometimes, and the people I care for may come and go.

But the love that you have left here in my heart means tonight I'm by myself but not alone.

I am learning, how love can keep you warm, how love can turn night into day.

I am learning, how love can keep me safe when I'm ever so far away

Days go by like the wind sometimes

Days blow by like the wind sometimes, and the things that I've worked for will come and go.

But the faith that you have helped me to understand, will help to smooth out the roughest road.

I am learning, how faith holds me up, when I'm too tired to stand on my own

I am learning, how faith takes the fear out of the darkness, and how it can help to guide me home.

Days go by like the wind sometimes.

Days blow by like the wind sometimes. The strength of my will may come and go,

But the hope you have given me will help to guard my dreams, and assure me that I won't get too old to grow.

I am learning, how hope is bound to faith and how together they strengthen your soul,

I am learning, how hope protects my spirit when pride and discontent try to take their toll.

Days go by like the wind sometimes.

Days go by, sometimes without noticing,

Days go by, sometimes in the blink of an eye,

Days go by, sometimes with a terrible quickness

Days go by like the wind sometimes…

Days go by like the wind sometimes…

Most people understand that time is fleeting. Anyone who has ever lost someone important to them in an accident or by someone else's violent act knows that the world can turn on a dime. The older we grow, the more we see of it. For a while, even knowing that, I still did not take the time to tell people in my life how much I loved them. I believe that once you embrace the fact that death is not an enemy and begin living each day so that you have little, if anything, to regret later down the line, the happier you will become.

I invite you to tell those people in your life that you love just how much you do love them. It doesn't have to be all sappy and sticky. Just a simple I love you and a hug sometimes works miracles all by themselves. Now there may be some people in your life that require a slightly more grandiose display and if it doesn't bifront you to give that little bit extra then, by all means, let them feel like they are the most important person you will have contact with that day. Me, I'm not one of those types of folk.

For me, it could be as simple as somebody telling me, Hey, I really do appreciate you, and I'm glad to have you in my life...and here's a million dollars...

...DAYS BECOME YEARS...

I know it sounds simplistic, but I'm finding it to be truer all the time. Words have power. Words can be constructive or destructive. Words can reflect the damaged you or the healing you. Words are either impulsive or intentional, and each can have a dark side as well as a light side. Words in response to anger or pain, often impulsive, run the risk of including past experiences in their generation; this would be a dark impulse. Words that are intentional that is, words carefully selected to elicit a specific response or purpose, can also be dark if the intention is to create further discourse. And yet, both impulsive and intentioned statements or responses can be filled with love and support.

In understanding ourselves and our influences on others through our words, it becomes our charge to always find the light from which to speak. In a lot of cases, that means recognizing the darkness in you and trying to overcome it before speaking. This is where feelings and understanding the real causes of those feelings become important.

(...oaky, after I wrote the following paragraph and read it back to myself, I'm a Freud it sounds a bit ....doctor-ish? I decided it would sound a lot more impressive if you would please read this with a German accent...trust me...)

Zo... it seems to me that feelings are reactionary responses, impulsive by nature. Feelings can be immediate or a slow burn. For some, negative feelings can steer their entire day in a bad direction if they let that negativity cause them to outwardly express that feeling. Generally speaking, if you are experiencing a rapid onset of negative feelings, it is likely that whatever is causing this "new" feeling is tied to more "old" feelings that were never properly dealt with and have been stacked on top of one another.

This "tower" of feelings becomes a threat to you with regard to your personal relationships. If you build a tower too tall it will eventually fall over. Imagine a toddler with building blocks. Sometimes, their beautiful, fragile towers crumble. Sometimes, that disappointment is overwhelming, and they throw themselves to the floor in tears. That tantrum is the child giving in to their feelings and allowing them to have control of their physical being. As adults we are rarely in a position to allow that type of behavior because we know that it would have a negative effect on everyone around us as well. What does this mean, it means we must find a way to address our feelings to prevent them from becoming that tower, an avalanche of negativity, a threat to ourselves and those we care for.

That being said, who hasn't wanted to throw themselves to the floor and kick and scream because of some moron at work, or because your spouse or teen-aged children have obviously lost their ability to understand English and simple directions? Remember, I am not a doctor... I don't even play one on TV. I'm just writing about what spins through my pointy little head and looking to share it just in case somebody else needs to hear it. I think it is pretty simple: your feelings ARE valid, but you really must self-evaluate them before you let them speak for you. As for me, I have noticed that probably 80% of the time... or more, if I allowed my internal, immediate response to any negativity placed in my way to be my first actual response, it would only serve to exacerbate the situation, leaving more hurdles to overcome later down the line.

When I was raising kids, teenagers to be precise, I noticed quite often that there was zero time taken between thoughts when they were angry. At that age, sadly, there is a physiological reason for shortened thought (... or no thought). You see, the frontal lobe of the brain does not become fully formed until we are in our early twenties. And that is where thoughts and emotions are formed. So, essentially, kids are brain-damaged throughout their formative years, which is why we, as adults, must attempt to stay vigilant in our responses to them when they are losing it over something dumb. I would ask my kids to take a minute and think to themselves, "... Is this thing that I am so upset about going to still be affecting my life in a day, a week, a year?" If you can see that it will likely be unimportant to your future, then just be disappointed, not angry…" That reasoning was my last line of defense against their wildly impulsive behavior. Sometimes that worked… sometimes not; they were teenagers, after all… you know…brain damaged.

So then, what of intention? I feel like intentional behavior is more like your intellect and/or your faith, molding your future. Our lives are filled with intentions. Some we follow through on, and some, not so much. Such is the way of the world.

We can indeed experience impulsive behavior where an intention is concerned. Say you are trying to impress someone you have more than a passing interest in…you know…your…horny. In your intention to impress, you do something impulsive, perhaps because you feel like there is a sense of urgency, and you do something that you have given little thought to before you actually did it. Your stunt backfires, and you look like a dolt. Such is the gray area between impulse and intention. Earlier in the book, I spoke of the "contemplation of consequence." This gray area is where perhaps a little more contemplation is required.

If you have done any research or reading about metaphysical stuff, then you are likely at least familiar with the concepts of the Laws of Attraction, the silent power of Expressions of Gratitude, or the practice of Setting Intentions. (… Look out, more hippie stuff is coming…) While I cannot claim to have a guide for anyone to follow, I can claim this: for me, finding a balance between the three above-mentioned concepts has indeed placed me where I am today. Contemplating these concepts and putting the thoughts to work that were generated in doing so is the reason this book now exists.

For me, allowing—no, asking—my mind and my spirit to pave the way ahead is the spiritual definition of intention. By practicing faith and doing my best daily to consistently give energy to positive thoughts and actions, I believe those energies can indeed act unencumbered by my doubts and fears and help draw to me that which benefits me most.

Days Become Years   *(09/2019)*

Day after day, became month after month, became year after year, lost in thought of time spent.

Breath after breath kept the cycle in motion, kept feeding the notion of a need to repent.

To study, to read, to write of my purpose, perhaps in the verses my freedom to find

Was no more than an accounting of the fears that were mounting, so subtle this poison, the slow-killing kind

My body, my spirit, and my mind had all fractured, not broken entirely, but damaged for sure.

Yet I always fight back, each time a bit weaker but determined to strengthen and do more than endure.

Always searching for light, for signs to be followed, awareness is slowly re-writing my script.

I believe in the miracle of my very creation and the removal of barriers over which I once tripped.

Close my eyes, stake my claim, call my future by name. I am the artist I hoped to become

My voice and my vision cut through all derision, to the ears, to the eyes, and the minds one by one.

With gratitude growing, every breath ever stronger, every thought ever clearer, I now live my intent.

To do more than observe, be more than just present, to be that for which I know this soul was meant

To sing of human foibles while I still have a voice, our foolishness reflected in the words and melodies.

To coax laughter at what makes us fallible humans until our collective laughter gains its perfect harmony.

So there is my answer, my antidote, my medicine, penance notwithstanding, my "Aha," my fix.

To live in this world and not let it consume me, to be aware and involved but not lost in the mix.

To share myself, both shameful and shameless, with anyone willing to hear

To bare myself, both fearful and fearless, giving up demons I once held so dear

Days become years, no stopping that progress, but I see now how quickly time can slip away

So, I pledge to myself and the giver of gifts to be mindful and grateful and not waste this day.

I do indeed wake up every morning, and if I am not in a state of gratitude, I will do my best to put myself there, often before my feet hit the floor. And while I can talk a great game about it, the reality is that some days are more challenging than others. I have found that in the long run, the greatest show of gratitude you can have each day is to be aware of wasted time. And then, when at all possible, make every effort not to waste that precious gift. Time is one of those rare things in life that you cannot buy, and you cannot possess more of. We may see money as an energy to utilize, but time does not. Time has no use for worldly things.

...DOG DAYS...

So, I live in Florida, where the average summer temperature is somewhere between 85 degrees and melt your sunglasses to the dashboard. My current breathing problems keep me indoors because eighty-five to ninety-five percent humidity, along with melt your sunglasses to the dashboard, makes it feel like I'm trying to breathe underwater. I mention this because my angel of a brother, Clyde, is currently in my backyard mowing my lawn. He is almost five years my senior and still can do this. God Love Him...

While he is doing that, I am sitting at my computer researching various crowdfunding programs to hopefully help keep me writing, singing, and creating art for the foreseeable future. He said taking care of my yard was a therapy of sorts for him and his way of supporting me in my quest, I love him...

So, we are here, in the dog days of summer, and in recent years, even born and bred southerners are trying to determine if it may have been someone in their lineage that is responsible for this heat we are experiencing...I mean, maybe they had a great uncle twice removed who did somebody's daughter and took off, or tampered with another man's wife...or livestock, or pissed off a witch or something. The point is it really does, from time to time, feel like a malevolent curse, almost as if the entire planet were getting hotter...

Even the alligators won't get out of the water.

Anyway, what follows is words to a song that has nothing to do with what you just read, other than the title....

117

Dog Days   *(06/2010)*

The summer's wearing long now, feels like these dog days just might last forever

Think I'll dig myself a hole and lay down, and hope that it helps me to weather this weather….

Whether it's going to work or not, I just can't say. It seems to work out just fine for my old dog…

Perhaps this dirty cool can keep my blues at bay

…but I just don't know; perhaps I never will

   Lord, I just don't know, perhaps I never will

My Yankee angel, she's done gone away, headed back up home, says that's where she needs to be

She said she couldn't breathe down here but I'm afraid, it weren't so much the heat as it was my stupidity.

I think I'll dig that hole a little deeper and drag myself inside. I'll try to bury that fool with the jealous bone.

And then perhaps from my blues, I'll no longer have to hide.

… but I just don't know. Perhaps I never will

   Lord, I just don't know, perhaps I never will

Winter's chilling wind is still a long way off, and already I am colder than I've ever been before

Don't think my apology is going to be enough, to bring that angel and her warmth back to my door

And I would truly love to promise, I won't be that fool again

But then that would just make me quite the liar, and everybody knows

Liars don't get any special friends…

....so I just don't know. Perhaps I never will,

Lord, I just don't know. Perhaps I never will.

No, I just don't know, perhaps I never will,

...perhaps I never will...

So, there was a guy who let his impulsive behavior mold his relationship with his woman. She opted to leave his sorry butt, and now he is wondering if he can repair the situation. He probably won't even try because his new level of self-doubt, coupled with his guilt, is already forecasting the worst. It will prevent him from trying and that assures the reality he may never know.

No matter what it is, you are getting ready to say or do, stop, think, take a minute to contemplate, and avoid regret later down the line. What is that old saying...you can't put the toothpaste back in the tube?

Lest I forget to mention it again, my brother Clyde, by way of handling some things that are currently beyond my capacity to manage, has, by his actions, shown his love and support for me and my dreams. I entreat you all to do the same thing. I don't mean to help me with things I cannot do. The fact that you have purchased and are now reading this book IS truly an act of love to me. But what I meant was to find something you can do for someone in your life to show them that you love them and appreciate them. It does not have to be a life-changing gesture (like becoming a monthly supporter to a struggling artist); just one that improves even a single day in someone's life is a great start.

..."YOUR WORLD" VERSUS "THE WORLD"...

So, I started writing this page on the following day from the previous chapter, three separate times during the day. Each time I started, I was interrupted by one thing or another. When I returned to my keyboard and re-read what I had written, it sounded very rehearsed and well-planned and not completely on track with where my mind was originally. Except for the third time that time I came back to my computer to discover that it had turned itself off. After a reboot, it was clear that my work had disappeared completely. I had neglected to turn on the autosave function.

And much to my chagrin, now I do not even recall what it was that reminded me of what follows. So, I'm going to save this now, and...

...wait a minute...HOLD THE PRESSES...

I remembered what my original inspiration was...oh happy day...

So, the original inspiration that caused me to remember the following little essay was hearing someone say something that, while being humorous, was still a rather passive/aggressive complaint. I was in a little bar and grill, catching happy hour and an early supper. In the booth behind me were two guys having a few beers before heading home from work. They spoke about work, wives, and kids, having a go at each other in a friendly albeit sarcastic fashion. One guy leveled a dig at the other, and the retort came back, "...look, I don't have to sit here, spending my hard-earned money on this lousy food, and take this kind of abuse from you. I could go home and get lousy food and be treated like this and for a lot less money."

...Man, where is the love?

So, with some regard to Dog Days, and in conjunction with the happy hour tete-a-tete, I offer the following thoughts...

Your World versus The World *(09/2023)*

Alright...the time has come... I have dusted off my soapbox, and I'm ready to speak the truth as I know it. I want to talk to you about love. I don't mean hippie-dippy-free love, man. I mean the love that nurtures, the love that provides spiritual sustenance, the love that is supposed to recharge us at the end of our weary days. For the last two decades, I have watched civility in my community, this country, and the world as a whole slowly erode to the point where we find ourselves now. An awful lot of people are exhibiting less patience, less willingness to help a neighbor, and less willingness to even be accepting of others in general. I am not talking about politics here; I am talking about our humanity. The most frightening part of this lack of civility is not only happening "out there" in the big bad world, but it is happening in our own homes. The very places where we are supposed to feel safe and loved are far too often becoming places of fear, anger, clenched jaws, slamming doors or just plain hateful language.

In the last few years, I have watched multiple relationships around me fail miserably. Rarely was it because of some singular, big, unforgivable action. Nearly all of these couples grew apart because they had forgotten what it was that caused them to fall in love in the first place. The "big bad world" was allowed to poison their minds so completely that they began to forget what "their world" was. Becoming so consumed in the negativity of the news and social media, or the negative portions of their workday, that they forget "their world" was there at home with the one, or ones, they loved.

Sure, sometimes it is drugs, alcohol, or infidelity, but even those things are rarely overnight situations. Someone, or both someones, changed slowly over time until the relationship became unrecognizable from its beginnings. I am one of the blessed few who had a very long and loving marriage. Of course, we had arguments, but we never forgot what we loved about each other. Often, the underlying issue in an argument was to help the other remember those things, thereby seeing where they were slipping away from that love and then trying to love them back into that knowledge. But I see a lot of people just giving up because they have lost faith in the world. You must remember that "your world" is not the same thing as "the world." Unlike the world, you can mostly choose what your world is like. And if you choose to let the world poison your world with hate, mistrust and indifference to the feelings of others, then all is lost, and our collective worlds will fail too.

As for me, I practiced and will continue to act, as my grandfather suggested, when speaking of how a proper marriage should work (and it is work...). Now, I know some roles have changed since the mid-1900 but the general philosophy still rings true. He said a man's task in a happy marriage is to make his woman's world as beautiful a place to live in as possible and to never let her forget she is loved and cherished. Her job in turn, reflects that love back to him, shares that beauty with him, helping him to see how remarkable their world is.

Ever heard the phrase, ...make your corner of the world a better place? Well, that is our task, folks. We should be doing our best to make "our" corners of the world, home and work life, better places to live in, places that prop us up, not tear us down. Now GO...make the world a more loving place to be...   ...start with yours... make apologies, kiss a little ass, find the blessings you already enjoy and express gratitude for them, hug each other, and laugh...for God's sake LAUGH!!

While the overheard happy hour conversation made me laugh a little under my breath, it also reminded me of conversations I had been part of with workmates before when they complained about going home from work. That never made any sense to me as I was almost always delighted to go home after my workday. I mean, a couple of decades ago, the majority of negative speech between friends was about some personal issue with work, money, or how a spouse or a kid ticked them off.

ow, it seems as if "politics" is always the elephant in the room. Do you see this too? Around the water cooler, at breaks during work, at lunch, in bars, restaurants, parks, you name it, you will hear disgruntled voices happy to place the blame for the majority of life's disappointments squarely on the shoulders of a government they are not happy with. A lot of people can't seem to help themselves and regularly find a way to interject politics into any conversation they can, just so they can vent some more.

Look, studies have proven that, without a doubt, what happens in the home for children to see and hear REALLY does have long-lasting influence on all of their relationships and decision-making throughout their lives. Knowing that this IS true (uh-oh, opinion time, boys and girls....), don't you think we need to be more diligent than ever in NOT carrying all the outside negativity of the world with us into our homes? We should be truly mindful not to load the air around us with negativity, anger or frustration. I've heard members of my own family wake up angry with the world because of current circumstances in their lives. The key word here is "current."...all things change, and if you can develop habits to remind yourself that you are a miracle unto yourself and more powerful than your circumstance, then you have a fighting chance to change your circumstance for your betterment.

Part of my mornings usually include some sort of personal affirmation. I have written many, so many, in fact, that I can no longer recite all of them every morning. Like any other new habit you try to create for yourself, you will miss some days, a bit like backsliding on a diet. I'll just share a few here.

I am

grateful for what was and lessons learned, I am

I am

grateful for what it is and the blessings I enjoy every day, I am

I am

grateful for what is to come, both the blessings and the lessons, I am

In order to gain a truer focus on my own growth, I ask that certain things be removed from me,

Remove from me my fear of lack.

Remove from me my fear of change.

Remove from me my fears and anger rooted in my past relationships with toxic people and places.

Remove from me the habits of procrastination and the self-generated doubts about my own abilities.

I am

more powerful than my circumstances, I am

I am

deserving of my dreams and the abundance it requires to enjoy them, I am

Amen

...ANXIETY, DODGEBALL AND HAIKUS...

I woke up a little too late to make the drive out to the beach and watch the sunrise, but a little too early to get out of the house for much of anything else. So, coffee and the internet it is for a bit. As is my habit (which is much in need of altering), I'll check social media, a bit of online news, and a couple of sites dealing with food, science, or music... I'm looking for anything that will crack the shell of my self-involvement. Over time, I've discovered that I have to get out of "my head" to see what is trying to influence me, good or bad. When I was in the 9-to-5 world, this type of morning would also include a variety of work scenarios, usually all looking at some perceived failure or, at the very least, the possibilities therein.

I'm certain there is probably a clinical name for it, but my train(s) of thought is occasionally an endless stream of one-liners. Rarely is there a theme tying them together. They could be about anything... jokes, politics, religion, recipes, sex, music, eggs, shoes... almost as if the inside of my head were the internet and I was skimming over all of the available rabbit holes at once. I know I mentioned it before... that, to me, this is creative ADD, and with a second cup of coffee, ADHD. If I hang around in my own head for too long with no direction, I'm dealt with the anxiety of how to break free from it, a bit like a person with autism getting over-stimulated and having to find a way to self-soothe. So, I try to keep an eye on the clock while surfing, and if I suddenly realize I've lost track of time, I stop immediately, get up, and walk away.

(...that is, of course, assuming that I am dressed in front of my computer. If I'm not, well, let's just say that self-soothe has more than one meaning...   ...sorry... ...TMI?)

Moving on...then I wander about the house, doing little things, pretending I am being productive, until my mind snaps back into place and gives me a real direction. It could be laundry, dishes, paying bills, practicing guitar, vacuuming, hell, sometimes

125

it is even writing. One particular morning in 2020 birthed this....this....thing.

Anxiety, Dodge Ball and Haikus   *(08/2020)*

Once again, I woke up "on the job," as it were, with nothing but deadlines spinning around in my head. Lost in a whirlwind of rhetorical questions...how can I, and...what if, and...can't we just...

When what I need are concrete solutions to the questions that are passed down to me by others who care not to think about them anymore. What the hell would make anyone think I want to do their thinking for them...anyway. I don't even enjoy doing all my own thinking... this is no way to live.

All of my big dreams are still just that ...big dreams... All of my intentions to change the way I live my life are challenged by the reality of my current debts as well as the monetary and physical limitations I currently operate from. I am working hard to see beyond those challenges.

At the moment, my sole survival is rooted in doing a job for someone else where my paycheck is my reward. Please don't misunderstand me. I like my job, and I even love the people I work with and for; we are a family of sorts...but it is still a job. For as much as we love one another, if I were to suddenly be gone (...and I know they would miss me), they would find another to do what I do. That is as it should be. Of course, it would probably be a bit of a downgrade for them, but they'll figure it out. And not all of my anxiety is rooted in my "working for a living," not by a long shot.

One of those big dreams I mentioned earlier is having the time and money to pursue "my art" in all of its loving, frantic, clumsy glory. The real issue: my soul's survival is often under attack by the anger, the attitudes and sometimes the actions of a great many

126

people whom I have never met, who do not even know who I am and yet have formed an opinion about the way they think I think.

This is one of those mornings where unchecked anxiety could have me feeling like the last man on my team in a game of dodgeball. I can see that the balls all have labels: politics, religion, anxiety, guilt, illness, poverty, hate, responsibility, fear... I feel I am subjugated to hear that resounding "PWANG" as the balls find their targets and leave their cross-hatched marks upon my flesh. Clearly, the other team members are all looking to make a headshot...and some days, it feels like the older I get, the more of them there seems to be. Some days in this wretched game of survival, the illusion of safety starts to look a lot like the fetal position...

But understand this: my trepidation is not about simply being hit. I have learned to deal with taking the hit from time to time. My fear is more about the confluence of my age, my health, the loss of earned retirement security, and whether I can still take being hit relentlessly, as it sometimes feels. Can I protect myself from being targeted by unknown attackers, who operate out of malice, with extreme prejudice...hit in the face... repeatedly...rendering me unrecognizable in my pain?

The truth in this matter is I must not lose my focus in the myriad of minor defeats I must deal with as an aging and as yet unknown artist. My protection has always been my sense of humor, my strength has always been my faith, my heartfelt reflections have always been found in my art, and I feel more inclined than ever before to share those reflections. In order to do just that, I must stay on my feet and, even in my instability, try my best to maintain a focus. Why? Because it is practically impossible to create art from the fetal position...

127

My muse is crying
  My heart bleeds for those that won't
    She knows that it hurts

My muse is grateful
  I am working to hear her
    She is working too

My muse gives me paint.
  Colors I don't recognize
    She says paint your fear

My muse is loyal
  Urges me to love harder
    She promises joy

My muse will not stop.
  She knows my soul is weary.
    She says I must try

My muse is tender
  We hold each other tighter
    Forging light through love

There are many times when I find myself writing something with little preparation and even less of an idea as to what is about to appear on the page. I don't mean my eyes rolled back in my head, mouth agape, making zombie sounds as I type. I just mean that sometimes, one sentence can quickly become two or three pages by the time the one sentence is fully examined and explained. It sometimes feels like I've been granted a Q&A with the divine as I ask the same question in a dozen different ways to arrive at an answer.

I am always fully aware that my answer is not the only possible one. But I truly love the moments when this "write it as it arrives" style suddenly uncovers a little something that maybe I needed to learn about myself.

As self-centered as it sounds, when the feeling of some sort of basic truth seems to have evolved, you can bet money that when it happens, I'm damn sure going to share it...warts and all. When I do, it is certain to be met with many different responses. Sometimes, for some people, it becomes an invitation to see what else I may have to share, and sometimes, for some people, it is the last straw, and we part ways. That is what is risked sharing your whole self with the world...

That is why when I purchased the domain name for Marginal Prophet Publishing, I also purchased www.wtfonline.net for future use. But in this case, WTF does not mean what one would first think. In this case WTF stands for Willfully Threatening Friendships, something we all do when publicly speaking our mind. I believe that the site may host a blog and open forum discussions of its own not confined to literary topics.

...THIS GUY...

In recent weeks, on and off, I have thought about doing a little traveling. I think about just jumping in the car and going... somewhere... anywhere, within a day or two from here. Find a pleasant place to hang out for a few days and see what there is to see. Maybe I'll meet some new people, find a Mom-and-Pop Diner for most of my meals, and get to know them a little. Perhaps actually getting to know some of their stories and finding inspiration for myself along the way. When I started thinking about where I might go, I was reminded of what most of my traveling had been like for me in the past.

A few years ago, I traveled for work fairly often. I really did not enjoy it very much at all. I would fly to a city and check into my hotel, including all transportation, generally that was an eight-hour day or more. Day two would be the actual job, inspections, and meetings, and sometimes a late flight home. Otherwise, day three was like day one. I rarely, if ever, got any time to visit any other places in a given city. While I was traveling, I tried to make notes for myself about impressions I got from people and places. But when all you see is the inside of buildings and airliners, surrounded by strangers, inspiration is thin at best.

Then came a day when I wound up with a two-and-a-half-hour layover that ended up lasting almost fifteen hours. I finished reading a book I had brought along. I finished finalizing my notes from the trip. And then, I sat there for an hour or so before deciding to get up and walk around.

As I walked from terminal to terminal over and over, I kept notes on my phone's voice recorder, describing what I saw. I even made up pretend scenarios for some people I observed. I was shocked at how many of these people were having affairs with co-workers.

When we finally got back in the air, I listened back to my recording and made more notes in a spiral-bound notebook that also goes on every job with me. Then, I promptly forgot it existed until my next trip six weeks later. So, throughout that next trip, I created the following… Fifteen hours of delayed jetlag make for dark places emotionally.

This Guy   (02/20)

I don't know how to be this guy,
what could be joy is often lost in flight,
emails, messages, conference calls, worry keeps me up at night.

Out of towner, I don't sleep,
haunted by the promises I'm employed to keep,
I'm forced outside of my comfort zone, but it's not in faith I leap.

Waiting to board, bored out of my skull,
a layover is not an actual lull,
a fraction of time in thousands of lives, where real lives are void and null.

Older men with tired faces
languishing in these waiting places
staring hard at younger moguls and hoping not to fall behind.

Slip-on patents, bumbershoots,
bulging valises and wrinkled suits,
no room is left for their boyhood dreams in such harried, cluttered minds.

Businesswomen, warriors, yes,

power players in tailored dress,

purely professional in boardroom shows, except for that which they dare expose.

To them, a compromise is normal,

even though the business pretends to be formal,

Still selling themselves as well as the job long after the deals are closed.

For some this life is all they know,

preparing briefs for the next big show

always on the run until at last,

they must let themselves fall down.

Their life is strewn on the second bed,

in the hotel room where they lay their head

then perhaps a drink in the airport while they're waiting to be leaving, again.

I am one of them from time to time,

in a sea of actors, mostly mimes

walking hard against the wind, that to others can't be seen.

I check my meds, and I'm praying hard

that my angel is not too tired to be on guard,

I'm beginning to see these lives we live as the darkest of tragedies

Travelers, both young and old,

some seem normal, some outside the mold,

all these lives are dependent upon the promise that someone has done their job

Thrown together in these places,

dodging looks from other faces,

feeling safe in their technology, this frightened, harried mob

Me in jeans and tattered shoes,

fighting with an artist's blues,

I write my story in hurried glyphs as other's deadlines approach

I'm wondering if what I am being paid,

Is worth the cost of a life waylaid

Plenty of time to contemplate as I eat pretzels back in coach

I'm not depressed. I just flirt with gloom,

a tightening time frame always looms

I press others for their stories as precious hours pass

Most will reply with platitudes

trite responses to indifferent moods

like language is exhausting to them, and conversation a pain in the ass

I search for signs of humanity.

To report them to others so they may see

Searching in other's tunneled visions for the glimmer of a soul

At best, I can tell you what I feel

And even that is a risky deal

Words that are seen as weapons can engage the ire of trolls

So I'll just tell you what I've seen,

as we root about for the American dream,

I've seen us more as conscripts or politely indentured slaves

We are paid, but just enough

to go into debt for things and stuff,

while the makers of the madness entreat us to be brave

"Work hard and gift us with your trust,

if you want to succeed, you really must,

it's the only way for you to surely get ahead."

When, in truth, the trap was set long ago,

before we began this come and go,

when to our father's fathers, the great lie had been fed.

I've no plans to become legendary.
With my thoughts, sometimes incendiary
my fervent hope is to light the fires in the hearts of those seeking peace

To speak out against the greedy all-consuming
to warn against the destruction that's looming
to beg mercy for this planet that we don't own but merely lease

So what to do now,
combat this somehow?
I tire of this fucking game,
but the fucking game pays my rent.

Not a leader do or die
Not a seer with a telling eye
I've only words to tell you
that my willingness is spent

I feel as though I should be carrying signs
When into a crowd again, I'm resigned
Some witty verses, some thoughtful memes,
some dagger of truth in all caps

But my placard is here. you're reading it
If I knew what to do, I'd be screaming it
But all I feel is frustration compounding,

and I fear an impending collapse

Today, I'm feeling trod upon
A hapless cog, a helpless pawn
The system being what it is,
today has the best of me

I've many more questions than solutions
From where do we attack these institutions
Such a limited choice of options
to set this country free

We live our lives in hand-me-downs
while they sport a brand-new tux.
Our backs support the tables,
where they set a feast to sup

We scramble for the scraps below them,
outstretched arms with empty cups…
Perhaps we could turn their world upside down,
if all at once…we just…stood up.

Okay, I don't know that I really have a follow up thought for that, since the original thought was about maybe traveling for FUN! To be honest, I came close to bumming myself out with that one. By the way, I still don't have any answers to our problems except to keep loving one another, hugging one another and finding something to laugh about.

But you'll notice before my rant/poem? I said I might drive myself on this potential pleasure trip. Flying is cool, but unless there is a once-in-a-lifetime opportunity waiting for me at the end of the line, I would rather go slowly and absorb the beauty that surrounds us all while it is still around.

I love the idea of watching as the geography changes around me when on a road trip. I love the idea of planning a day's travel to include some park somewhere or some amazing natural phenomenon like waterfalls or rock formations. I love finding myself going through some small town and discovering they stake a claim to the best barbeque in the state or that some diner has a sandwich named after a medal-winning Olympian because they was born in that town.

I mean, c'mon, from the air, you probably can't even see the world's largest ball of twine at all...

..SELFISH PRAYER...

I have offered you as readers some of my fauxlosophies about the world and our places in it. I hopefully have told you enough through my stories that you are aware of the sort of person I am. I have told you of some of my own shortcomings in educating myself in the quest to live MY life as I wish. It has taken me a while to discern that there is a difference between living a life you are contented with and living a life you are in love with every day. I am still working on that for myself, and drafting this book was my first BIG step in revealing myself to "the world."

Putting my thoughts into writing and starting a website with a series of blogs and videos sharing my art is what I have felt I should be doing for a very long time. I just had a hard time launching myself into it. Sometimes it was financial and sometimes my own ethic, where facing my responsibilities was concerned that held me back from really trying. I'm embarrassed to say that I had a very hard time shaking the thought that everything had to be perfect before it was released into the wild. Now, probably because of my age, I don't really worry about perfection any longer. I only worry about getting it all out of my head before I croak.

Over many, many years, I got used to being the support that my family needed. It was the right thing to do. It was the honorable thing to do. I was living a life mostly contented but with little extra anything for myself. When I was getting close to the time when thoughts of retirement started seeping in, I realized I had little idea how to not be a working stiff.

When I decided that I could start being somewhat selfish with my time and my money, I also realized that I did not know how to do that either. My wife supported me and my dream to enter into retirement years as an artist. But I still entertained some guilt in learning how to be selfish for me, and she really could not help me find my way around that guilt. Many of my prayers and meditations around this time had to do with God and the universe at large assisting me in clearing the way for my new desires and goals.

Well, now I'm going to share one more thing with you of a very personal nature. I was hopelessly in love with my wife, a woman who sometimes had a hard time loving herself. She came from a place where love was rarely given freely. It always came with some sort of price attached. Toward the end of her days on this planet, she became darker, quieter, more reclusive, if you will. A mild substance abuse had something to do with that, but it went deeper than that, and I could not seem to help her. I could tell you the whole story, but why…you will understand the picture as it is drawn. It was many months before I could begin to shake the guilt of the story that follows and know that some days it still vexes me. But I feel it needs to be shared; once you read it, you'll understand...

Selfish Prayer   (06/22)

you may one day wake up wishing,

to take back things you said,

when you learn that what you whispered to the void,

still echoes in your head

one voice is saying, "…not your fault

you more than passed this test."

but the echoes come back loud sometimes,

regrettable at best

ripples from a pebble dropped

vibrations active still
grow waves of doubt and sadness
that taste of bitter pills

she waged a war inside herself,
and in weaker moments, I became
the enemy in effigy,
to memories, she would not name

I tried to be her champion,
I loved her endlessly
but pain removed her passion,
and left little there for me

yet every moment we shared, loving
found a place to stay in me
it hurt so much to want her
when she could not let that be

I mean, I will love her always,
in me, she will always be
that fearless girl of endless light,
that helped to set me free

but she lost faith in a simple fact,
that she was a blessing to all she knew

and I fought for her not to forget,
but inside her, a darkness grew

...so I gave God an ultimatum
in pain, these words I uttered
in frustration, demanded changes
in selfishness, I muttered

"I'm tired of this battle, Lord,
I'm tired of the fight."
"...tired of punching holes in the darkness
to let in a little light."

"I just want her to be happy and
I can't seem to help her see."
"I can't fix her, Lord and if you can't either,
then please take her from me."

now I know it was an illness,
silent, strong and old
that took her from this world and me,
and left her body cold

but still, sometimes, I wonder,
was I stupid to be so bold
as to challenge God in my selfishness,
to do as he was told

my faith tells me she is happy now

she's as whole as she will ever be

and I feel there is a knowing grin

when she looks down to see

I've no regrets about our time spent

the laughs and tears we shared

but now that she is gone... sometimes...

I regret my selfish prayer.

The first two lines of that poem reflect my coming to an understanding that all words and thoughts can indeed grow to shape our reality. Did my words shape the outcome for her? No, her illness was years in the making and well hidden. She was confronted with the notion of dealing with not one but two illnesses that could take well over a year and a half to recover from, that is if she could recover from the surgeries and therapies. She could not bear the thoughts of becoming fragile, helpless, and becoming a burden to her family. In the space of just a few days, she declined at an alarming rate and was gone.

But we had a shared view of what life after death meant. We mourned death but were certain that the next adventure was destined to be a great one. We always tried to find the blessings in everything that was presented to us. Now, I can smile every time I think of her, which is explained in the next offering.

She was a rather competitive individual as well and always said she would be the first to go. I guess she took that "until death do you part thing" a little more seriously than I...

...VERY LONG GOODBYES...

So, that last one was kind of beautiful and awkward at the same time, wasn't it? Sometimes, baring yourself to the world in your art is uncomfortable, and sometimes it is downright frightening.

This next one has been considered a little "iffy" too by some of my friends. But for me, the lyrics you are about to read were me attempting to celebrate all that I loved about being in love with my late wife, Pat. I have told folks before, when they offer their sympathies to me, that I appreciate them but do not need them. We had 48 loving years together. Where would I get off being sad that it could not have lasted longer? Some people never know that kind of love...offer them your sympathies.

It took over a year to write this song because, at first, no matter what I wrote, it always came out sad, and I did not want it to sound like a sad song. And oddly enough, this song's first few lines were written before her passing. Needless to say, they took on a different meaning after.

Now that she is gone, I no longer need to ask permission from her to entertain my selfish side. I get to fuck things up on my own terms, and that is remarkably freeing. But at the same time, I know that she is still in my corner. She is still around sometimes, watching over me, probably rolling her eyes at me from time to time. There have even been a few times when I swear I hear her say,"...really, Shawn?"

Very Long Goodbyes   *(10/2021-11/2022)*

Saying goodbye in the morning if you still laid there in bed
Meant touching you one more time as I kissed your sleepy head
Tracing lines, I knew so well, my fingers wanting more
Well-worn thoughts of all those places that I'd grown to adore
Sometimes, that made for a very long goodbye
An extra squeeze, an extra kiss, one more look into your eyes
As much as I hated leaving, we both knew it was what I had to do
Those long goodbyes lasted me all day until I came home to you

Some days, I'd pour us coffee as I headed out the door
You'd come shuffling down the hallway in your robe and not much
more
You'd throw your arms around me so tight I could barely breathe
I felt your warmth against my chest, and that made things hard for
me

At times, we lingered in the doorway, one last kiss before I went
Your love stayed wrapped around me no matter how my day was
spent
And every time I had to leave you, I made certain that you knew
Not only was I still in love, but I still lusted for you too
Sometimes, that made for a very long goodbye
An extra squeeze, an extra kiss, one more look into your eyes
A flash, a smile, a giggle, never knowing what you might do
Those long goodbyes lasted me all day until I came home to you

When came the night of our last goodbye; you spoke of what was to be

How I should take this second chance and do what's right for me

You said go and play your music; you've a new life to be found

Be bold and live it happily. Don't you dare just sit around

A nurse called to say that you had passed just as I was getting home

I felt your love run through me before I picked up the phone

Had I been there at your leaving, I might have begged for you to stay

I'll suppose the Lord knew better than to string us on that way

God knows our love made for very long goodbyes

And you knew I was not strong enough to watch you leave this life.

But our long goodbyes will comfort me, even now that you are gone

Those long goodbyes now proof to me that the love we shared lives on

I'm glad our love made for very long goodbyes

An extra squeeze, an extra kiss, one more look into your eyes

A grab, a grope, a giggle, never knowing what you might do

Those long goodbyes lasted me all day until I came home to you

  I am grateful for our very long goodbyes

    I thank God for you and our very long goodbyes

      Yes, I'm glad. Our love made for very long goodbyes.

So, the last two offerings, I think, show two sides of a coin where love is concerned. A long-term relationship is going to have difficulties occasionally. There will be times when doubt, anger or frustration will be present. And therein lies the keyword, the "present". If you have been paying attention in your life, you already know the quote, "…this too shall pass…" It is so true; nothing lasts forever. But if you choose to hang on to those negative feelings of the present, long term, then shame on you. Long term, those negative emotions damage you and your spirit.

And if you are the one whose behavior has sparked those feelings, and you have been doing it long term, then the shame is at least doubled for you, and as the agitator, you better realize that you risk losing it all by testing the ones you love. Love is always a work in progress, but it should absolutely not be tested for its durability by pushing the limits of patience or trust with the one you say you love.

And long term relationships are not just about marriage. They are also about friends, siblings, your children, and those you work with or for extended time frames. And all of those relationships will have their moments. So, I suggest again to all of you out there, remember what drew you to these people in the beginning. If the attraction was real, organic, and brought you joy or affirmation in more than a strictly physical sense of some sort, then hold on to that even when things get "iffy." And if you cannot remember what that initial draw was, chances are it wasn't real to begin with and may not be what is best for you now. You can ask your friends or family for advice on such things, but a decision on that matter cannot be made by anyone else but you.

...WHY DO YOU LOVE ME...

As long as I have your attention, and I am still thinking about relationships and what it takes to make a good one, let me share this: we sort of covered honesty, intimacy, kindness, selflessness and sex, but there is one more thing...humor. You absolutely must maintain a sense of humor. Being able to find bright spots in otherwise dreary days and give your partner a giggle is the best way to beat the blues. In almost any circumstance (notice I said almost...), there is a chance for humor, even if it seems misplaced at the moment. I have been blessed or cursed, whichever way you choose to see it, with the gift of inappropriate laughter, so was my wife.

We were those people that you really didn't want sitting next to each other at a funeral, or in a courtroom, or in a theater, for that matter. We found so many things to laugh at, and often at the strangest of times. And we thought so much alike that one of us would often warn off the other, already knowing where their mind was headed. Then, even the fact we were sharing the same silent, twisted thought could be enough to set us off.

The following little story happened around Christmas time, and who knows, you may be actually reading this around Christmas time...

So....MERRY CHRISTMAS

...c'mon, stranger things have happened...

Why do you love me?   *(12/2019)*

Why do you love me?

147

My wife Pat had asked me this question before, and if you are in any kind of serious relationship, I'd be willing to bet your significant other has asked you the same question before as well. As badly as I want to help her understand, this has never been an easy question to answer without sounding mushy, pervy or downright stupid. Well, today, I finally have the answer.

All of my children are now living out on their own, with some little things left behind here and there. And as we find these things we set them aside until we fill up a box, and then we will bring the box to them. Often, as she was placing something in the box, I would see her pause, and I'd see her get that "my baby is all grown up" tear in the corner of her eye. I love her for that, but that does not say anywhere near enough about how loveable she is. For that matter, neither does referencing her body, her cooking, her intelligence or the sex..

But... this evening, as I was taking some boxes of stuff from my house to my son's house, I had my epiphany. It was already dark outside. I was carrying the last thing to the car, and my wife followed me to open the car door for me. I did not even ask for her to do so. See there, thoughtful, another reason to love her. As I kissed her goodbye, I looked up at the house and remarked on her hard work in lighting the house for the upcoming holidays.

"Your house looks really fuckin' cute, babe," I said.

"Yeah, it really does," she replied.

"Just like you sweet cheeks," I said as I groped her butt before she could step away, "...I guess the big difference is I don't want to have sex with the house".

As she walked away, she was slowly shaking her head and said, "...I don't even know how to process the things you say to me sometimes..."

"And that's why you love me," I chuckled. I got in the car and started the engine. I put on my seat belt, turned on the lights and began to back down the driveway.

My peripheral vision told me she was still standing in the open front doorway. I looked back up at her, expecting a little wave or her blowing me a kiss. And sure enough, there she was, cute as anything...as always... well illuminated by all the Christmas lights she worked so hard on.

She stood there holding onto the doorway, leaning away from it with her back arched, leaning back as far as she could with her head back, shaking her hair from side to side as if she were a model for some luxurious hair product. She completed the image for me with one knee up in the air, dry-humping the door jamb.

...and THAT, my friends, is why I loved her...

Thankfully, the private side of our relationship was filled with small surprises like that quite often. Those truly unexpected little things always feel much like when a relationship is new, and surprises come easy as you learn about one another. A good relationship isn't so much about perfection as it is the willingness, each day, to remember why you love who you love and do something to remind them of it, too. I guess that what I'm trying to say is wanting to make that effort for each other and often is all important.

When it comes to your lover/partner/spouse, never stop courting them. Do everything that you can to keep passion alive between you. That means more than just sex or sexually charged actions. Soft, occasional displays of tenderness are essential. Say, I love you...say it often. Say it in different tones. Say it in private, say it in public, say it in front of people, say it when there is a quiet moment, and you are together, alone. Touch them when you say it, and touch more than just erogenous zones when you do. And maybe, just maybe, every so often, dry hump a door jamb for them.

...SALIERI STABBING MOZART...

Recently, I have been faced with looking at myself and trying to determine how I first perceive others I come into contact with daily. Without going into details, let's just say that multiple people in my life have vented to me over the last couple of weeks concerning people or circumstances in their lives that are making it hard for them to keep their relationship with a loved one healthy, or get ahead financially, or what is keeping their spiritual growth from moving in a forward fashion. And I told you before. I'm not a counselor, a fiduciary expert or a freakin' guru... And while all I could really do was be a sounding board for them, it did begin to pose some internal questions for me...

So why did that make me look at myself more closely? Because anytime someone begins to vent to me, I automatically feel that someone may be looking to me for advice. My brain feels the need to begin formulating advice to offer up, just in case. While that sounds innocent enough, I have to check carefully to be certain where MY advice is coming from.

Am I listening with my heart in an attempt to be empathetic first, hoping to better understand their pain or anger? Or am I listening to them with an analytic mindset to give a response right away? Am I listening with my guard up or down? Am I reflecting and projecting, or am I allowing myself to try and feel what they feel as they vent? Sometimes, just letting a person clear the sadness or anger from themselves is all they need to refocus themselves and gain a clearer perspective on their own troubles, and they don't really need my advice at all. At any rate, this renewed, albeit temporary, reflection on my own reasons for self-doubt reminded me of something I wrote a few years ago. And just a few months ago, I revisited it, and it became a song...go figure...

Salieri Stabbing Mozart   *(08/2020)*

You know I have my troubles, much the same as you.
And it kind of helps just knowing I'm not alone.
This morning, for example, I woke up feeling stressed
A mental state my spirit can't condone

So I wander in my bathrobe and my slippers
And I wonder why I cannot be at ease
My ethic should not drown me in its pathos
And my logic doing little to appease

For every answer I think I've found,
there's another question
Every question in itself is another clue
I am surely not a guru or a savior
Just another mensch who's trying to muddle through

More days than not, I'm waking up too early
Brain cycling through the things as yet undone
With backing tracks like Salieri stabbing Mozart
Like a carousel from hell, this ride is no longer fun

Spinning much too fast to score a stylish dismount
The ponies turn to gargoyles and grotesques
I think I could use some pills, or a very long vacation
Either way, it's clear I could really use some rest

For every answer I think I've found,

there's another question

Every question in itself is another clue

I am surely not a guru or a savior

Just another mensch who's trying to muddle through

I do not have the answers, but I've questions I will share

If you care to, you may use them as your own

But I caution you, my questions have a dark side

They are meant to question what of self is shown

Puzzling heads, for reasons that only souls possess

We're all piecing life together as we go

Make our mantras that of gratitude even under great duress

And pray for peace in the things we cannot know

For every answer I think I've found,

there's another question

Every question in itself is another clue

I am surely not a guru or a savior

Just another mensch who's trying to muddle through

Consider this a sign you may have missed along the way,

The truth may change over time and circumstance.

Consider this a gospel if you need one to reflect on,

Don't stop looking and leave it up to chance.

The search for truth is only half the battle,

You must also learn the source from whence it came.

And while you search, I beg you to remember,

That truth, like God, is known by many names.

For every answer I think I've found,

there's another question

Every question in itself is another clue

I am surely not a guru or a savior

Just another mensch who's trying to muddle through

It is becoming clearer to me all of the time that all of my self-reflection, and investigation into the human condition is what is shaping my personal fauxlosophies. I know, that seems like a pretty obvious thing, right? But if that is all it takes to foster a philosophy, that means any schlub can shape a philosophy. And if that is the case, then maybe, just maybe, all of these classical, well-known philosophers that we say we are learning from may not have been so special after all. Perhaps they were just as messed up as the rest of us are.

You know what else? Until now I never gave any thought as to whether there needed to be any type of proof to support a stated philosophy. I've been writing for years, and I consider some of what I have written as very informative or inspiring. I have written poems, songs, essays and one-off ramblings for decades, always wondering in the back of my head if my thoughts would have any relevance to anyone else other than me.

...I'm actually beginning to think that I may indeed be a philosopher to some degree. What I mean is while I did not study the subject anywhere, and I have read precious little of the classic texts available, I do have my own opinions on how and why people act the way they do. I do not ever recall hearing two people engaged in a lively philosophical discussion and hearing one of them shout, "...oh yeah, Plato....prove it!" have you?

Okay, now I'm feeling a little bit cocky about myself... I mean, now it feels like I may be overstepping a little... Here, I am calling out guys like Plato, Socrates, and Aristotle, challenging their historical status. If they were around today, folks like you and me might find ourselves hanging out in a bar with them having a beer, saying shit like, "...Oooo, check out the big brain on Voltaire. Or maybe trash-talking Pythagoras.

Yeah...I think I'll shut up now. It's starting to feel as though I could be just one Freudian schlepp away from disaster.

...LONG AND HARD...

In case you have not gotten the impression yet, I am trying, perhaps for the first time, in earnest, to re-create myself, my world, and my happiness. I have already been what "the world" said it needed me to be. And now, with the cooperation of the universe, I am going to try new things. I am going to experience new places, new people and new feelings. I am going to make art without worrying if it will be a success…that is up to others to determine.

(FYI ...if you guys are going to see to it that I have success, bless you, thank you...just know this: I would prefer money over fame...I mean, I can spend money)

Just in case it wasn't made evident by the fact that I have actually created a book, I have determined that I do, on occasion, have a poetic side that could be considered a bit classical. That poet occasionally slips off by himself and comes back with a cool idea or two. I don't ask him where he's going. I'm sure I don't need to know. That poet occasionally lives in tandem with my hopeful romantic side. From time to time they work together to create some wonderful things, some tender, warm impressions of human connection.

Sometimes, however, that poet goes slumming about with my lizard brain, my limbic lothario. And when it does, very different works of art are created. Sometimes, that work is still soulful, and sometimes it is just angry. Sometimes, this limbic-infused art is still loving, but sometimes, it is just plain lustful. Sometimes, the art reflects a willingness to grow, and sometimes, it only reflects a disenchantment with the world. Either way, from this time forward, I intend to allow that beast its voice, too.

Long and Hard *(08/2024)*

I thought long and hard about how it would happen
Me drafting a book of poems and such
I looked at some others. I flipped through some pages
They did not excite me all that much

Perhaps it was my lack of understanding
Where the poet hoped his visage would be landing
Anyway, my boredom notwithstanding
Sometimes, it seemed that forcing a rhyme was the poet's only crutch

I'd read a rhyme just for the sake of rhyming
I'd spy a word whose only purpose was for timing
Or there'd be a line of no consequence,
and no overarching theme

A challenge to my willingness,
to offer second chances
Like the author was just killing time
as he chased a fading dream

At times, feeling like a pattern
had been lost or maybe scattered
Sometimes, changing like it didn't matter
This left me the rank outsider to some members-only scheme

Perhaps you, like me, in the here and now
Are trying to determine exactly how
I'm going to tie together,
all the muck that you've just read

I'm not sure that I know how
to bridge the voids created
But I hope that in the final lines
I can satisfy your head

I hope before your brain shuts down,
a saving grace herein is found
A message to take with you,
that will serve you in due time

One poet to another,
place your bets and spin the wheel
And face the fact that sometimes,
a poem is just shit...

...how do you like me now?

So, I know... I rather misled you. You were probably thinking things were about to get sexy up in here...yeah? Well, consider this "literary sleight-of-hand."

Do you think I owe you an apology?

I can accept that... I find it easy to apologize. It doesn't hurt me or my self-image to do so, and if it makes you feel better, then

I am happy to help out. Just know that there will NOT be any refunds or retractions where my self-expression is concerned. As I grow older, I find I care less about what people think of me with regard to fitting into a mold of any sort, even the mold of someone I may have been in the past. I set my intentions long ago to be a working artist.

Well, I'm here. I am an artist. I am going to speak my mind from time to time. I may, on occasion, create work that is witty, insightful or downright profound. On the other hand, I may create a work of such remarkably trite banality that it might make one wish to slap the mediocrity right out of me.

Did you ever hear the old saying, "…if you're going to be stupid, you'd better be tough"? Well, the artist's version of that could be something like, …if you are going to make art, then you'd better be prepared to suck...

Why?... Because that is absolutely going to happen from time to time.

There will be artistic fails; there has to be, or it is a sure sign that you are not stretching your artistic muscles nearly far enough. My followers will not see all of my failures. First of all, it would take way, way too much time to cover them all. I mean, failures are a bit like warts or hairy moles. I can tell you I have some, but I doubt if you would actually want to see them all.

But I can tell you this: where my failures are concerned, if I learned anything important as a result of them, you can be sure that at some point in time, I will be able to use that knowledge, I will share, I will talk about it.

...FARE THEE WELL...

So we have made it to the end of this book...together.

After years of directionless writing of poems, essays, and bloggy notions, then months of confusion in trying to determine how to share them with the world it all came down to this...

I don't know about you, but the end kind of snuck up on me. I hope you found some things of interest as you read along. I hope you found some beauty in some of the words. I hope you found some things that allowed you to think beyond a box you may not have fully appreciated you were in. I hope there were a few laughs along the way. Mostly, I just hope you enjoyed yourself while reading.

I'm sure some of you along the way were trying to figure out what kind of person I am. I am certain I was confusing at times. But hey, I feel pretty confident that occasional confusion on my part, could lead to new thoughts on your part, thoughts you've never had before, and maybe that is a good thing. Same sort of notion as when you are working out physically and you introduce "muscle confusion" into the mix. Suddenly, the same muscle groups you are used to dealing with in a particular way have to act differently than they are accustomed to. That is what leads to a more complete workout and, eventually, a more complete physique.

I hope that is what I have been able to do for you intellectually or spiritually. I had fun with this, and I hope that I get to do it again.

...FINAL THOUGHTS AND ASKS...

I humbly ask that you bear with me during my growing pains as a "new creator" within the arts and the ever-expanding digital world. Even though I have been an artist of one sort or another for most of my life, it wasn't until recently that this analog dog began learning new tricks. Throughout this book, among other things, I alluded to being a singer/songwriter. Well, that is true, but again, as of the writing of this book, I have never actually gone to a studio to create fully produced recordings. I'm hoping that will change very soon. In the meantime, you can find some of me, my music and more at the following places, or just google shawn.eager1

https://soundcloud.com/shawn-eager-1

https://www.reverbnation.com/shawneager

https://www.youtube.com/@shawneager7162

Shortly after this book gets released, I will start a Patreon page for myself for anyone who cares to help support me in my artistic walk-about with monthly pledges for as little as a dollar a month. As time progresses and I learn more about staying truly connected in the virtual world, I do hope to hear from you. I will be creating additional tiers of support that will have exclusive content made available to them.

But without regard to monetary concerns PLEASE visit the page from time to time to see the progress. Just use my name when you go to Patreon's Homepage.

After "I Love You Anyway," I mentioned an "Earth Magic Mama" that I followed, well it happens to be my daughter, and you can find this ray of light at www.blessedmoonalchemy.com

Thanks Again...PEACE

© 2024 Marginal Prophet Publishing, LLC

Jacksonville, Fl.

www.ingramcontent.com/pod-product-compliance
Lightning Source LLC
LaVergne TN
LVHW051410080426
835508LV00022B/3018